THE HERITAGE OF JOHN CALVIN

Heritage Hall Publications, Number Two
Calvin College and Seminary Library

THE HERITAGE
OF
JOHN CALVIN

Heritage Hall Lectures
1960 - 1970

Edited by
JOHN H. BRATT

WILLIAM B. EERDMANS PUBLISHING COMPANY
Grand Rapids, Michigan

The essay "The Genevan Mission to Brazil," by R. Pierce
Beaver, first appeared in the *Reformed Journal*, July-
August 1967. Copyright © 1967 by William B. Eerdmans
Publishing Company. Used by permission.

The essay "The Intent of the Calvinist Liturgy," by James
H. Nichols, first appeared in the author's *Corporate Wor-
ship in the Reformed Tradition*. Copyright © MCMLXVIII,
The Westminster Press. Used by permission.

CONTENTS

PREFACE

When Calvin College moved in the 1960s to the Knollcrest campus, it entered on a new stage in its development.

With the building of a new library on the Knollcrest campus, a specific area in it was designated as Heritage Hall. At that time, a lecture series was projected—a series to deal with John Calvin, Calvinism, and related areas. Dr. William Spoelhof, President of the college, appointed a Heritage Hall Lecture Series committee consisting of Professors Lester De Koster, then Director of the Library (who later resigned from the Calvin staff to assume the editorship of the denominational weekly, *The Banner*); M. Howard Rienstra, of the History Department; John Hamersma, of the Music Department; and John Bratt, of the Religion and Theology Department. The President also served on the committee, *ex officio*.

A number of distinguished scholars were invited to the Calvin campus in the 1960s. They brought the rich fruits of their study and research, and the Calvin community is much indebted to them.

By grant of the Calvin Foundation, whose generosity we hereby acknowledge, the findings, observations, reflections, and judgments of the scholars are being made available to the general public in this volume of lectures. With a few of the occasional references excised, these lectures are substantially the same as what was delivered in Heritage Hall.

We commend them to you with the prayer that John Calvin's God—who is also our God—may be praised through these scholarly efforts.

John H. Bratt

7

I

JOHN CALVIN: DOCTOR ECCLESIAE

JOHN T. McNEILL

In Ephesians 4:11 we are told of the gifts of Christ to the church in the ministry, in the ranks of which are apostles, prophets, evangelists, pastors, and teachers. If you look this up in Beza's Latin text, you will read:

> *Is igitur dedit alios quidem apostolos, alios vero prophetas, alios autem evangelistas, alios autem pastores et doctores.*

Those who know the Greek better than the Latin will recognize that the word here used for teachers is *didaskaloi*. Calvin himself uses the expression *doctor ecclesiae*. It

John T. McNeill was awarded the Ph.D. degree by the University of Chicago in 1920; he also holds honorary degrees from Westminster Hall, Queens University, Edinburgh, and Paris. He has served as lecturer and professor at Westminster Hall, Queens University, Knox College, Union Theological Seminary, and the University of Chicago. He has contributed articles to Church History, Journal of Religion, Religion in Life, *and* Theology Today. *Among his books are* Unitive Protestantism, History of the Presbyterian Church in Canada, History and Character of Protestantism, *and* Modern Christian Movements.

9

appears in the title of *Institutes* IV,iii—"The Doctors and Ministers of the Church." In section 4 of this chapter he distinguishes the functions of pastors and teachers: "Teachers are not put in charge of discipline or administering the sacraments, or warnings and exhortations, but only of scriptural interpretation—to keep doctrine whole and pure among believers." And it is well known that in the Ecclesiastical Ordinances of 1541 Calvin set a distinct place for the ministry of "doctors."

Robert W. Henderson, in *The Teaching Office in the Reformed Tradition: A History of the Doctoral Ministry*, has followed the difficult course of Calvin's "doctor" through history. There has always been a tendency to combine in one person the doctor or teacher, who with academic learning declares the doctrine or teaching, and the pastor or preacher, who explains and applies it to the people. Calvin indeed did not object to pastors' being called doctors "so long as we know that there is another class of teachers (*alterum doctorum genus*) who preside in the education of pastors, and in the instruction of the whole church" (*Comm.* Eph. 4:11). The tendency to merge the two offices is nowhere better illustrated than in the case of Calvin himself, who was equally employed in the pulpit and in the academic chair. In both offices, but chiefly as teacher, he vastly extended his impact on mankind through the printed page. In what follows we shall try to confine our attention to his exercise of the doctoral ministry.

In Roman Catholicism the term *Doctor Ecclesiae* is a title applied to about thirty teachers of special distinction. By various popes from Boniface VIII on, these have been named and commended to the schools of the Church as guides in theology and ecclesiology. In recent decades numerous Roman Catholic scholars have turned with a new appreciation to Calvin, and there is every reason to think that this trend will continue. We have of course no expectation that he will qualify for the papal accolade; but he has already accredited himself as an eminent teacher to a great part of the Christian church. Not the least remarkable phenomenon of the twentieth-century theological scene has been a new scholarly attention to Calvin's great body of writings. It is no exaggeration to say that during the past half-century the image of John Calvin has grown before the eyes of the entire Christian world of thought to a stature never before reached. His works written—and his work achieved—are coming to be judged more appreciatively, and he is known by those who knew him not. Thus the designation "Doctor of the Church" may be more confidently applied to him today than it could have been formerly.

It is useful to remind ourselves at the outset that Calvin's teaching took its rise from a deep personal experience. Of this Calvin said little; it may not have crossed his mind that readers centuries away would wish to know more of his inner motivation than he incidentally disclosed. But certainly—like Paul, Augustine, Luther, and countless other eminent Christians—he passed through a crisis of conversion, the effect of which gave character to all his later thought and effort. It was long after this happened that he first wrote of it in direct and explicit terms: "God by a sudden conversion subdued my heart to teachableness." In this familiar sentence, have we duly felt the force of his word "teachableness"? Heart and intellect were alike quickened and redirected. Looking back, he declared that before this divine intervention came to draw him out of the mire he had been stubbornly attached to the unreformed papacy and that thereafter he burned with zeal to pursue new studies centered in the Scriptures. He soon began, we know, to put together the materials for the first edition of the *Institutes*. It is clear from this and other autobiographical fragments that Calvin the theologian and teacher of the church came to his office by way of conversion and that this involved a protracted and painful inner conflict. Clearly, too, he was very much aware that it was

God who took the initiative. We may regret that he was not more communicative on the details of this transforming experience. He had so much to wrote about God, God's word, and God's church that he chose to be reticent about himself.

The man whom God subdued to teachableness and directed to new studies found in Holy Scripture the central documents of his intense intellectual labor. In this task he does not scorn the aid of the church fathers or of the pagan philosophers before them. Indeed, he seems to have taken every author in his vast range of reading as a potential teacher and useful stimulator of his own thought. But he rests his teaching constantly on that of the Bible. The sacred Scriptures were inspired by the Holy Spirit and the devout reader is aided by the Spirit in comprehending their meaning. In this sense, the Bible is the word of God. Something mystical or sacramental is involved in the Christian use of Scripture. It comes from God the Holy Spirit; and its message is made available by the work of the Spirit whereby it is self-authenticated to the mind obedient to the Spirit, and is not to be subjected to reasoned proof. Superior to all reason is the inner testimony of the Spirit. Yet, if reasons are asked, Calvin will furnish reasons for accepting the divine authority of Scripture. It surpasses the greatest of pagan writings and "is crammed with thoughts that could not be humanly conceived" (*Inst.* I,vii, viii).

Calvin is far from regarding all parts of Scripture as of equal value, and nothing could be more erroneous than the notion that he relies on the Old Testament. This is evident from the fact that he wrote commentaries on most of the New Testament books before his first Old Testament commentary appeared in 1551. His references in the *Institutes* to New Testament passages (4340) are almost twice as numerous as those to the Old Testament (2424), despite the disparity in length of the Testaments themselves. He does firmly believe in the continuity of the Old and New Testaments, but he devotes a chapter to the superiority of the New with its fuller light and its range of concern for all mankind in "the calling of the Gentiles." Indeed, the Old Testament receives its significance for him by its anticipations of the New (*Inst.* II,xi). Incidents and rites recorded in the Old Testament are taken as "types" or foreshadowings of what was to be made clear in the New. Moses and the prophets had as their task "to teach a way of reconciliation" leading to the reconciling work of Christ (*Inst.* I,vi,2); and "the inner testimony of the Spirit" needed for an understanding of both Testaments is a testimony to Christ. "The ancient prophets spoke by the spirit of Christ," and it is the passages lending themselves to this interpretation that Calvin cites most frequently. For him the whole Bible is primarily a book about Christ. Still, his commentaries show an extraordinary grasp of historical facts and a power of historical imagination.

The Scriptures are inspired, but Calvin does not make them verbally inerrant in the fashion of modern fundamentalists. When he speaks of the apostolic writers as "authentic amanuenses of the Holy Spirit," the context speaks of doctrine and not of words. Commenting on II Timothy 3:6—"All Scripture is given by the inspiration of God"—he remarks that the law and the gospel are "a doctrine . . . dictated by the Holy Spirit." When it comes to words he does not hesitate to admit errors: Paul, following the LXX, has used a defective rendering of Psalm 51:4, and in repeating the words of Scripture the apostles were *saepe liberiores*, often pretty free, for they were not shackled by a *religio verborum*, a scrupulosity about words. It is the teaching (*doctrina*) that is divine, not the mere words. In his commentaries Calvin treats the words of Scripture often in detail, but as a humanist scholar would treat them, in search of their natural meaning.

No doctor of the church, not even Chrysostom, of whose work he makes much use, was more consistently and effectively than Calvin a doctor of Holy Scripture. He began in Geneva as lecturer in Holy Scripture, and he played this role to the end. Within his works we find embodied the most systematic and penetrating exposition of Scripture that the Reformation produced. Calvin thus gave impetus to the progress of biblical research and interpretation that has continued through the centuries since his time, with its exciting developments in our age. We cannot tell what attitude he would have taken to this or that trend in contemporary biblical criticism. He might have found in some of it a lack of that "piety" and that reliance on the Holy Spirit's guidance which he thought essential. But we should not forget in this connection his warning against the rejection of any truth, even from pagan and secular writers. "If we regard the Spirit of God as the sole fountain of truth, we shall neither reject the truth itself nor despise it wherever it shall appear, unless we wish to dishonor the Spirit of God" (*Inst.* II,ii,15).

Calvin, the doctor of the church, presented a doctrine of the church that remains perpetually challenging. In his last letter, written to his old co-laborer Farel, he takes some satisfaction from the fact that their labors together have been "useful to the Church of God." It is readily inferred from the language he uses in referring to his "sudden conversion" that this experience was difficult because it was a crisis of church attachment. It meant his departure from the papal Church to the ranks of the evangelical party. In the *Institutes* and in the Ordinances of Geneva the outlines were drawn of the Reformed church that was beginning to take shape. But for Calvin the church of God was a far more vast and more spiritual entity than any visible church, whether of Rome, Zurich, Wittenberg, Canterbury, or Geneva. It was the "holy catholic church" of the creed; and the phrase that follows—"the communion of saints"—was uniformly taken by the Reformers as a description of the holy catholic church. It implies for Calvin "that the saints are gathered into the society of Christ on the principle that whatever benefits God confers upon them, they should in turn share with one another"

(*Inst*. I,iv,3). He excludes here any required community of worldly property but stresses the sharing of spiritual goods, especially of the confident awareness of saving grace.

The distinction between the church, which is truly catholic, one, and holy, and the external and visible church, which is found to be defective in holiness, is clearly drawn; but Calvin's great urge, and we may say that of the Reformation, was to bring to the visible church the holiness and the oneness that are the properties posited of the Holy Catholic Church. For that which was reformed in the Reformation was the visible church, which, as the Reformers saw it, had been left in the previous age neither One nor Holy nor Catholic nor fit to express the communion of saints. Among the Reformers it was Calvin who most clearly and emphatically voiced these concepts.

While Calvin often assails in unmeasured terms the corruption and superstition of the unreformed papal Church and urges complete withdrawal from its worship, he nevertheless does not for a moment think of himself and others in the Reformation as presiding over the inception of a church that had not existed before. The church of all God's people has never ceased to exist. It is ageless and indestructible. Even within the confines of the visible unreformed church there have remained vestiges of the true catholic church, like a half-demolished building (*Inst.* IV,ii,11-12). Thus "the visible Church which is also Catholic" has an element of continuity through all times. Calvin with Cyprian and Augustine calls the visible church the mother of believers, who, he says, are conceived in her womb, nourished at her breast, guided and instructed by her throughout life. While we recognize that not all who within it make profession of their faith are truly of the faithful, we are to exercise "a judgment of charity" among them.

The marks by which a true church may be discerned are the true preaching of the word and the right administra-

15

tion of the two scriptural sacraments, together with true discipline, by which the sacraments are protected from profanation. It is sinful to depart from a church showing these proofs of its reality, even though it may embrace members whose lives are scandalous. The churches in Galatia and Corinth had among their members crude offenders, yet they were not sweepingly condemned as false churches. A visible church of perfect saints is excluded by the fact that we believe in the forgiveness of our sins. The visible church is not a community of perfection but a community of forgiveness, whose members daily pray "forgive us our debts" and are daily forgiven (*Inst.* IV, i,21-23). Knowing their imperfections, Christians strive onward, advancing in holiness but not attaining in this life to sinless perfection.

Calvin was indeed jealous for the sanctity of the church and its congregational life. In this spirit he gave attention to the reform of public worship. The forms he introduced and his explanations of worship were calculated to impart a genuine experience of the holy, a sense of common participation in a holy action and in a fellowship of saints. Incidentally, in this connection he strictly enjoined kneeling in common prayer (*Comm.* Acts 20:36). It should always be remembered that Calvin's whole system of discipline was primarily designed to guard the sanctity of the Lord's supper, which ought never to be profaned by the presence of scandalous offenders. The Geneva Articles of 1537 already make this clear: "such good discipline that none may present himself at it (i.e. 'the Holy Supper of the Lord') save holily and with singular reverence" (Art. 1).

To nourish and guide the church, God has provided a ministry. We shall not retrace here the steps of his argument as he tries to establish from Scripture the four orders or offices of ministry that he would see employed: (1) the preaching pastor, corresponding to the presbyter or bishop of the New Testament; (2) the doctor or teacher; (3) the deacon, who serves the sick and the poor; and (4) the elder, who joins the minister in the government of the church and the administration of discipline. Great emphasis is placed on the function of preaching as being primary in the work of the early bishops and presbyters, who were required "to feed the people with the Word of God" (*Inst.* IV,iv,3). To this end the minister must be equipped with sound learning. One of Calvin's most memorable sentences occurs in one of his Sermons on Deuteronomy (5:23-27). *"Nul ne sera jamais bon ministre de la parolle de Dieu sinon qu'il soit premier escolier."* No one will ever be a good minister of the word of God if he is not a first-rate scholar (or, perhaps, a competent student). We remember what zeal and labor Calvin expended in the establishment in Geneva of that famous Academy, which soon became an international institution of high renown for its work of supplying ministerial leadership to the Reformed congregations in many lands. The opening of the Academy in 1559 was the fulfilment of a long cherished plan; for in the Ordinances of 1541 Calvin had written of "the need to raise up seed for the time to come, in order not to leave the Church a desert to our children" and of "the obligation to prepare youth for the ministry. . . ." These words are echoed, by the way, in the foundation documents of Harvard University.

I have not cited the entire sentence. The additional words are "and for civil government." Calvin saw these two functions, that of the minister and of the political leader, not as being in antagonism but in balance, and he made provision for both to be prepared by means of the best possible education. Augustine, Aquinas, and Luther had written on civil government before Calvin. In fact a great deal of the accumulated literature of political theory had been the work of scholarly clergy. Calvin thought so much and with such deep concern of things political that he devoted to civil government the final long and searching chapter of the *Institutes.* And here he finds another

17

"ministry," for the magistrate is a minister of God for the peace and welfare of the people. Calvin's political concern was intense and had to do with every part of Europe. But this in no sense means that he entered a secular realm out of harmony with his religious interests. It is true that he was a trained lawyer and in an early treatise had shown familiarity with the classical writers on government. But for Calvin the churchman and theologian, every man in all circumstances of life, no less than within the precincts of the church, has a transaction, an unceasing business, with God (*negotium cum Deo*). So one of his first official utterances in Geneva states that the rule of kings and magistrates is something holy, *une chose sainte*, and that they are to be obeyed as God's appointed lieutenants. Men who are not concerned with "the public good of the country where they live" are unfaithful to God, and rulers are required to do nothing unworthy of their office as ministers of God. These ideas were later expanded. The relationship of ruler and ruled is brought within the Christian law of love. Magistrates on their part are "responsible to God and to men." The coercive power entrusted to them is to be exercised under God's authority and with the clemency that Seneca praised. In this frame of motives they may resort to war to protect their people and may levy just taxes, never forgetting that their revenues are the very blood of the people. Even un-Christian and even unjust rulers are to be obeyed, except where they command us to do what God forbids.

Calvin at first showed no preference among the three forms of government discussed by classical writers, monarchy, aristocracy, and democracy. Like Aristotle, he discussed the deviations or perversions of each of these. But he introduced into the *Institutes* in the edition of 1543 a clear statement that in his opinion "aristocracy or aristocracy tempered by democracy far surpasses the others." The aristocracy-democracy pattern was well exemplified in the constitution of Geneva, which Calvin helped to revise in that same year. It was not an aristocracy of lineal descent. In one of his commentaries (on Micah 5:5), written in 1560, he views hereditary kingship adversely as out of accord with liberty; and other utterances of his later years seem to show a growing rejection of monarchy. In 1559 he explained his preference for the aristocracy-democracy combination on the ground that kings lack in themselves the ability and justice to meet their duties, so that it is preferable that a number (*plures*) bear rule together, helping and admonishing one another and together restraining rash and aggressive individuals. In different contexts Calvin speaks feelingly of "the inestimable gift of liberty," and liberty is an important ingredient in his picture of good government, a treasure to be prized and defended, indeed "more than the half of life" (*Opera* XXIV, 629).

Without sanctioning armed resistance to tyrants by unauthorized individuals, he does from the first hold in view that restraint of kings exemplified by the ephors of Sparta, the demarchs of Athens, and the tribunes of Rome. These ancient functionaries he takes as typical of "popular magistrates" whose responsibility it is to protect the liberties of the people against oppressive rulers. He sees this function properly exercised by the Three Estates of existing realms, an allusion that I take to be, *inter alia*, an appeal for a meeting of the French Estates General (which had not met in his lifetime) to assert authority against the Valois rulers. In these fragments of Calvin's teaching we see some reasons why many of the Calvinist tradition have been contributors to the spread of liberty and of government by and for the people.

If Calvin viewed the function of government as "a holy thing," he wanted likewise to bring a religious and Christian tone to the marketplace. It is very easy to go astray in the interpretation of Calvin's economic ethics, especially when the subject is approached with secular presuppositions. Certainly he does not regard worldly prosperity as a

19

reward for, or a consequence of, a godly life. "We see daily," he notes, "the state of the faithful is more miserable than the state of the despisers of God" (*Comm.* Job 42:7). The view of Job's monitor Zophar that a man in prosperous ease is in favor with God, Calvin pronounces as "the error of the Sadducees" and the product of "the devilish error that men's souls are mortal" (*Comm.* Job 21:7). And he explains "Godliness is profitable" by saying that the faithful who are vexed with afflictions are in their extreme poverty happier than the despisers of God, because they are assured that God is with them. His works abound with such observations, though this is not observed by the school of Weber. We cannot discourse on this tempting theme at this point: suffice it to recall that, among others of his time, Calvin led away from Aristotle's notion of barren money and from the Old Testament literal prohibition of interest and permitted strictly limited interest on loans for production. He would have the whole of economic life controlled by the principle of stewardship. Everyone should consider that "he is a debtor to his neighbors, and that he ought in exercising kindness toward them to set no other limit than the end of his resources," which ought to be expended according to "the rule of love" (*Inst.* III,vii,7). From such passages (and they are numerous) any fruitful study of Calvin's economic ethics must begin.

Calvin warned against that asceticism which would despise the good gifts of God by which our physical life is enriched and rendered pleasurable. Food and drink are given for delight and good cheer, not merely for sustenance. "God has clothed the flowers with the great beauty that greets our eyes, the sweetness of smell that is wafted upon our nostrils. . . . Did he not distinguish colors so as to make some more lovely than others? . . . Did he not endow gold and silver, ivory and marble with a loveliness that renders them more precious than other stones? Did he not, in short, render many things attractive to us apart from their necessary use?" (*Inst*. III,x,2). E. Harris Harbison has rightly called attention to "the idea of utility in Calvin's thought." But because of his intense feeling for God's handiwork in the created world, Calvin sets beauty above utility. Calvin was a man fascinated by what he likes to call the "beautiful theater" of the created world in which we do well "to take pious delight," meditating on nature's phenomena as of God's creation (*Inst*. I,xiv,20). Even in the animals we may contemplate the majesty of God. He calls attention to the beauty of the horse, the hawk, and the dove, and notes that the lowly ass participated in the splendor of the son of God. One could take from Calvin an extended anthology of passages eloquent of the world's beauty, always with reference to God, the Author of beauty, often uttered with regret that these tokens of God's majesty are set before sin-blinded eyes (see Léon Wencelius, *L'Esthétique de Calvin*, chapter XI). One is prompted to ask whether the artist or the poet who disclaims the desire to delight us with beauty falls into this mood because he has first lost his sense of God.

It is not required of a *Doctor Ecclesiae* that he be infallible. But he must be both learned and dedicated, an exemplar of what Calvin's friend John Sturm called "*pietas literata*." "True piety," Calvin wrote in 1537, "does not consist in a fear that would gladly flee the judgment of God [but rather] in a pure and true zeal which loves God altogether as Father . . . and dreads to offend Him more than to die." The first edition of the *Institutes* is described in its subtitle as "worth reading by all persons zealous for piety." Calvin uses the word "piety" with great frequency, and in its ancient, large and generous sense. It is a praiseworthy dutifulness primarily to God, motivated by reverence and love. It was this that was the mainspring of Calvin's life effort.

His labors were the astonishment of his friends. His mental energy seemed inexhaustible. To the heavy schedule of his lectures and sermons, unrelieved by vacations or "sabbaticals," were added his great array of published works, constant attention to the most demanding administrative duties and decisions, conferences with visitors and resident exiles in Geneva, and an extensive correspondence with people of every rank—kings and statesmen, learned friends and fellow-Reformers, and humbler folk in trouble. It is remarkable that in his letters he very rarely alludes to the overwork involved in all this. Despite bodily weakness and pain, he accomplished all this with a certain élan, a characteristic sprightliness of mind, and a promptness that is suggested by his Latin motto, *Prompte et sincere in opere Domini.* His brilliant and rarely matched gifts of quick perception and almost flawless memory continued unimpaired while his bodily strength slowly ebbed away. All his great talents were perpetually stimulated as they were exercised in the context of his piety. His learning and teaching rose to the measure of his devotion. *In opere Domini* nothing was to be withheld. Thus it was that for thirty years John Calvin drove at top speed the high-powered engine of his brain. Thus he became so great a teacher of the church that it is still after four centuries profitable for us to come under his instruction.

II

ST. THOMAS AND CALVIN AS
THEOLOGIANS: A COMPARISON

QUIRINUS BREEN

The indefinite article "a" in our title is intended to mean "one." The one comparison to be made between these two theologians pertains to method. In method St. Thomas and Calvin were as far apart as Plato was from Isocrates, or Aristotle from Cicero. For St. Thomas wrote as a philosopher, Calvin as a rhetorician or orator. In the history of literature, the *Summa Theologica* stands in the philosophical tradition, the *Institutes of the Christian Religion* in the sophistic.

Certain assumptions and distinctions must be made. To begin with, the method determines very largely what is

Quirinus Breen received the Ph.D. degree from the University of Chicago in 1931. He has taught at Hillsdale College, Albany College, Grand Valley State College, and the University of Oregon. He has served as a Fulbright Research Scholar, and has contributed articles to the **Oregon Law Review.** *His books include* **John Calvin: A Study in French Humanism; De Veris Principiis of Marius Nizolius;** *and* **Christianity and Humanism.**

said, but what is said by such eminent Christians as St. Thomas and Calvin aims at one and the same thing: an exposition of the Christian faith. From this it follows that the method, whether philosophical or sophistic, is not the faith content. The content of each pertains to the Christian religion, and each man is as warmly devoted to this as the other. If this is not agreed on, our discussion will be merely academic. If it is true that the method is not the faith content, it is fair to say that theology is but a way of discoursing about the faith. It is not the faith itself. It is important not only to grasp this, but constantly to live with this distinction. It can be readily appreciated how a full realization of it would increase a theologian's modesty; it would equally tend to reduce excessive chauvinism in the rival theological traditions. The Catholic who thinks criticism of the *Summa* calls the gospel into question would be as wrong as the Calvinist who equates criticism of the *Institutes* with doubt about the faith. In any case, for the purpose of this paper it is basic, for it aims to put Thomas Aquinas and John Calvin in the historical perspective of their respective literary traditions, so that each (but especially Calvin) may be more realistically understood and critically assessed.

Biographical study of great thinkers helps to understand them better. We comprehend Plato and Aristotle better if we take into account their lives as well as writings. Plato's *Letters* have things to add to our vision of him as a man, giving a context that is often neglected to his thinking. The report of Aristotle saying, as an old man, that "the lonelier and more hermit-like I become, the more pleasure I take in the old myths," makes one sense in him a quality too rarely appreciated. Spinoza as an old man is known to have found consolation in passages from the Old Testament Scriptures.

Do such biographical data cancel out anything these authors have written? Not at all; but they put them in such a new perspective as to feed wonderfully our imagination about the man and the book. So it can be with St. Thomas and Calvin. Actually, their own evaluations of their major works appear modified in this light. For both were first of all Christians, and as such personally involved in the faith. For example, as a Christian, Calvin labored incessantly for interfaith fellowship (largely with non-Catholic bodies); and in this interest he did not insist on his specific view of the real presence in the eucharist, nor even on his doctrine of double predestination. As a Christian he was more than his theology. As for St. Thomas, it is well known that after his ecstatic vision near the end of his life he said in effect that, compared to what he had seen in the vision, all he had written was as nothing. On his deathbed he really got down to basics when in his confession he spoke as a child of five. A man's total life is indeed greater than any part of it, more even than his life's work.

To say that theology is not faith but only a discourse about it is not to depreciate theology. To point up its importance, three things must be said.

First, when we theologize we discourse rationally about the faith. We do this because we are rational. The reasoning may be simple and superficial or deep and complex, but we have no choice but to act on some reflection. Historically, there are two aspects of reasoning about religion (and markedly so about a religion deriving directly or in good part from the Bible—whether part or all, to wit, Judaism, Islam, Christianity). We can reason about the faith (1) as to its satisfactions for the individual, and (2) as to its relation to the world. Scripture offers tests that suggest such in part, for example, "answer every man that asketh you a reason for the hope that is in you" (I Pet. 3:15), or "bringing into captivity every thought to the obedience of Christ" (II Cor. 10:5). Perhaps there are clearer passages; in any event, there has been in Christianity a powerful thrust rationally to justify personal submission to the faith and an equally powerful thrust to achieve a Christian world-view and culture. The modern historiographical concern with intellectual history, or history of ideas, has been showing what powerful, event-making forces ideas can be; and ideas about faith have been among the most potent. If the faith is as significant as we consider it to be, theology has an awesome responsibility to generate and organize ideas worthy of it, so bodied forth as to give substance for the imagination to feed on.

Second, theology has many forms of expression. If it is a rational discourse, it may be expressed in a *Summa Theologica*, but historically it has also taken the form of Bible commentaries (Origen), dialogue (Justin Martyr), poetry (Prudentius), sermons (Pope Clement I), prayer (St. Augustine's *Confessions*), essays (Tertullian), rhetorical discourse (Calvin). Besides, it is almost a commonplace among some literary critics to inquire as to theological ideas implicit or expressed in satire (Erasmus signed himself as Doctor of Divinity on the title page of his *Praise of Folly*) and in modern drama and fiction. In some of these, theological ideas are very subtly expressed, and the reader assimilates them often unconsciously, as by some osmosis. Theology, then, speaks in many literary tongues. The theologian should really be several persons, for some mastery of all these tongues is requisite for proper discernment of what is said in each.

Third, concentrating (as we shall) on theology in the philosophical and in the rhetorical tradition,* those who have a Reformed heritage have some advantage in sensing Calvin's doctrine of common grace. For if the Christian faith as such is not of human origin, philosophy and rhetoric are. As gifts of common grace, they have a charter of liberties to be what they are on their own terms. Being human, both philosophers and rhetoricians are liable to error; this is equally true of the theologian who speaks in the tongue of philosophy or of rhetoric. Being a "saved" man does not keep him from error when he uses philo-

* The same holds true for the other "tongues" or forms of expression.

sophical or rhetorical methods. As philosopher he is liable to violating the laws of coherence and noncontradiction, or to reason in a circle, or to have an undistributed middle, or to identify "some" with "all." As rhetorician, there is no guarantee that he will not argue like a prosecuting attorney disallowing a proper "devil's advocate" or paper over cracks in argument with colorful metaphors or shout and pound when heat seems more useful than the one-candle lamps available.

Calvin speaks both of the utility of these arts and of the arts themselves. His most eloquent language is devoted to their excellence, which is so great that he was "compelled" to admire them; and as gifts of the Holy Spirit they would not be neglected, much less despised, without contemning and insulting the Spirit. While it is his considered opinion that these arts have no eternal value, the fact alone that they are gracious gifts of God spells for him that not to honor them is sinful. And how shall one better esteem them highly than by knowing them as fully as possible? As for the usefulness of such knowledge of St. Thomas and Calvin, that will occupy the rest of this essay.

*   *   *

We shall speak of St. Thomas first. His philosophic method of theological discourse approximates the ideal of philosophical style, for philosophy should pertain to pure reason. Now his style would have been more purely philosophical if he had composed it in the form of Euclid's geometry. Spinoza did this in his book on *Ethics*. Descartes tried it. But St. Thomas did fairly well in aiming at the intellect alone. It is evident that this restricted the circle of his hearers or readers. St. Thomas taught in the theological faculty, having as students candidates for the doctoral degree. He did not teach that cross-section of society represented in the teen-age student body aiming at the bachelor's degree.

Moreover, the particular characteristic of his method is disputation, which characterized all medieval scholasticism, law and medicine as well as theology. Disputation took various forms, but ideally the heart of it was dialogue: living mind with living mind. The first use of this was in the University of Bologna's faculty of Roman law; St. Thomas did much to perfect its use at Paris (the quodlibetal disputations). The *Summa Theologica* is in disputational form. After stating the proposition, St. Thomas lists objections (1, 2, 3); then he says "on the contrary," which introduces some authority from the Bible, a church father, a philosopher (generally Aristotle), the Roman law, etc. Upon this he says "but I say," giving his own view. Lastly, he lists replies to each of the above objections.

The spirit of this method goes back to Socrates, especially as portrayed in Plato's dialogues. The Platonic dialogues opened a new era for the mind, largely through Plato's "discovery" of the rational soul and the force with which he made it a subject matter of philosophical discourse so that every return to Plato endows reason with a kind of pristine power and glory. It went something like this:

(1) The dialogues body forth a delight in analytical and speculative thought, not merely when it destroys naive, unexamined generalizations, but especially when it opens up vistas of promise for better things. This fascination and charm is recovered, even when only a little taste of Platonism is enjoyed.

(2) When the life of analytical-speculative thinking, inaugurated by Socrates in his marketplace encounters, was lived, confidence in the regenerating power of reason grew so much that it was held to be, so to speak, a way of redemption. Thus, to live by the motto of "know thyself" was not only a delight but it was a way of living a redeemed life. It added cubits to human stature to have a new and irrefutable way of understanding the distinction between man and brute. So great was confidence in it that

Socrates—and after him Plato—took on in their conversations all manner of men willing to reason. It was the Greek counterpart of a better-known invitation to "come, let us reason together."

(3) By practice, dialogue developed rules of dialectic; and Aristotle, Plato's pupil, added logic. That is, the rules of reasoning were projected, so that discussion might remain on the rational plane. So to say, this was a framework of discourse within which men of diverse orientations could converse so fruitfully as at least to discover things they had in common.

I will omit touching on the process whereby this Greek tradition reached St. Thomas, but surely he was a beneficiary of it. Delight in intellectual analysis and speculation marked him, say, in respect to the notion of being and contingent being, in epistemology, in exploring the meaning of the glory of God. He was so confident of the power of reason as to engage subject matters touching men of diverse orientations—not only Christians, but Jews, Moslems, jurists, businessmen. He was fortunate to come to maturity when dialectic and logic were accepted arts in the universities, arts that suited his temperament. Whether he was always right does not matter; the method is right. One could wish that all who pursue this method might bear in mind the entire quotation from St. Peter, "Answer every man that asketh you a reason of the hope that is in you *with all meekness and fear.*" Dialectic and logic can cut both ways.

In Greece, there was no important conflict of faith and reason. This came when some knowledge was held to come through revelation. St. Thomas made a memorable defense for the existence of faith and reason in the same man at the same time. To him the complete man is one in whom both are wedded, with each living in accordance with its nature. This is not always easy, and it is often not happy, if happiness is considered an uninterrupted romantic glow. But if happiness is completeness, it is a happy state. A parallel is the union of man and woman: not always comfortable, but it makes the unit of society, and as such is a completeness, and is therefore a happy state of existence.

To sum up in one sentence the significance for us of St. Thomas's method is impossible. A meaningful aspect for our present ecumenism is that he demonstrates the great force of reason in action. This holds immense promise. Should we fall back into our quondam separate states of self-satisfaction, St. Thomas has nothing to tell us. But new knowledge, the world situation, and, above all, the sinfulness of isolationist complacency have stimulated an unbearable hunger for reasoning together.

*   *   *

We come to John Calvin. To understand his rhetorical method of discourse, we must paint in some background.

To begin with, Calvin was not opposed to all scholasticism. Thus he defended Professor de l'Estoile who at Orleans taught him Roman law in the old scholastic manner. This was in 1529 when he had had a good taste of the humanistic method (under Alciati), and had turned away from preparations to study scholastic theology. It is not necessary to discuss here specific factors that made him disdain the scholastic method for theology by the time he began the first edition of the *Institutes of the Christian Religion* in 1535, but that he did then reject it as a theological method is evident.

However, certain things were in the air.

To begin with, William of Occam (d. 1349) had caused a split in the theological world. There were two major camps: those who had confidence in philosophical method as important for theology, and those who had little trust in it. Philosophy thus had become double-headed. This was serious, for now there was no accepted common frame of reference indispensable to dialogue. Besides, in general, the tendency was for many stronger minds to turn away from theology as a profession.

Moreover, the papal hierarchy had for two centuries been losing its shine. We need not here rehearse the story of the Babylonian Exile, the Schism, and Conciliarism. Nor do we need here to narrate how, in spite of some earnest efforts toward internal renewal, the results were not impressive. There was a growing distance between the hierarchy and the vocal lay world. In politics, the locus of authority was moving steadily to local princes or leaders and to national kings, who dealt with the papacy on *their* terms. The new education was enjoying an increasing appeal, especially to townspeople. While many hierarchs, also popes, were not out of touch with all this, there was no effective thinking on how the church should adjust to it, so as once again to have moral leadership.

It is to the point to say something of the new education. Stated briefly and too simply, the pith of the new curricula had to do with literature. This was the classical—first the Latin, then the Greek—but since the fathers of the church wrote largely in the classical style their writings were included. Interest in the Bible was also stepped up (the Septuagint and the New Testament had been produced in classical times). The movement so wholly concerned with a renewed study of ancient literature is known as humanism. The humanist was a professional scholar bent on literature-centered curricula in the old schools, and founding new schools where the old rejected the innovations.

Three concerns of the humanist are significant for our purpose: the revived literature as to content, form, and central aim or ideal.

The Renaissance concern with content may be roughly described as a kind of reverence for all literature that hailed from classical times. Humanists found in it much wisdom human and divine; it offered abundant historical examples of both good and bad conduct in politics and individuals. The fifteenth-century reappearance of the complete works of Plato was in many ways revolutionary (among others, for helping make a proper mental context for the Copernican theory; for raising the status of mathematics; not to mention the inauguration of more serious concerns with comparative religions as wisdoms). To suppose out of hand that Calvin's mental set was made without Platonic influence would be hazardous. Calvin's sharp break between the terrestrial and the celestial did not fall from the Platonic tree. We owe a debt to his religious genius and to his imagination that he operated constructively with the "break."*

But important as the content of classical literature was in the Renaissance, that concern itself was not as such characteristic of that era. For medieval scholars also had a certain awe for ancient literature (classical, patristic, biblical). This is seen in the twelfth-century Renaissance and more spectacularly in the higher faculties of the twelfth and thirteenth centuries (Justinian for law, Galen for medicine, Aristotle for theology), while the authority of St. Augustine continued, and of course regard for the Bible was paramount (St. Thomas held a "chair of Bible"). But three things mark this medieval concern with ancient literature: (1) it was limited, because of general ignorance of Greek; (2) its pursuit was mainly limited to learned men, not touching the average of the clergy and nobility, nor the townspeople (let alone the peasants); (3) with respect to Aristotle (to limit ourselves to him for the present purpose), prominent scholars (in time with papal protection) used him primarily for apologetic reasons aimed at intellectuals (whether Christian, Moslem, or Jewish). Besides providing Christians with a certain confidence that the faith was not contrary to reason, they intended to show that, say, the Arabs (like Averroes) erred in limiting the faith to Aristotle's views of God's relation to the universe, of the nature of the soul, and so on. But even so,

* See my paper on "Calvin and Humanism: His Doctrine of Common Grace."

medieval preoccupation with classical literature, especially Aristotle and Justinian's *Corpus Juris Civilis*, was so great that it helped prepare the European mind for reception of practically the entire body of extant classical literature.

More characteristic of Renaissance humanism was its concern with literary form. This had to do with textual and internal criticism, vocabulary, syntax, imitation of style, comparative literature, and so on. Concomitants were: the hunger for manuscripts, leading to laborious and sometimes exciting hunts for them; the demand for copyists; the growth of a competent critical scholarship greatly stepped up by the invention of printing with movable type.

All this (and much more) is what is meant by saying that Renaissance humanists were philologists. The first to exemplify this with distinction was Petrarch (1404-1474). Giuseppe Billanovich tells a story concerning a manuscript of Livy's history of Rome. A scholarly ecclesiastic wanted to read it for more precise information about the Romans. But when Petrarch got hold of it, he at once noticed how bad a copy it was. So he proceeded to make corrections, many of which were so good that later philologists could not improve on them. The next philologist of Petrarch's mettle was Lorenzo Valla (1407-1457). By the sixteenth century, north Europeans equalled them: Budé, Erasmus, Melanchthon, the Scaligers, Henri Estienne. How deeply young Calvin was involved in this is clear from his Seneca commentaries. This work was something of a declaration of faith in the Erasmian ideal of virtue through knowledge. As a Protestant he did not demit this view; he continued to regard the humanistic curricula centering on the new knowledge* as a way to make man better. How else account for the classical caste of Geneva's school? But

---

* Knowledge as to the content of classical literature, but through texts cleansed by philology; knowledge also in the sense of, so to say, becoming classical men, so far as emulation—if not imitation—of the clarity and elegance of ancient literature could effect it. The ideal was refinement: *homo humanus.*

there was a difference: the betterment through knowledge was of common grace, not saving grace. This latter is another matter altogether, upon which we must not here enter.

Along with content and form went the classical ideal of the perfect man. It is written large in the classical literature that man is a speaking animal. If Plato's ideal was rather that of silence and contemplative wonder, his defense of it was made in language that for power and beauty has not been surpassed by any master of speech. The prevailing ideal of manhood was the orator. The most eminent classical orators were considered to have been Demosthenes and Cicero. Each was the finest flower of his era: the Greek democracy and the Roman republic. To be an orator in the best sense, there must be free speech. When Greece lost her free cities, oratory became declamation, as it did when the Roman republic had become the empire.

Though the professional orators, or rhetoricians, no longer championed the cause of free speech, that cause was not dead. It was taken up by men possessed by the spirit of philosophy (especially certain Cynics and Stoics) and by men of religious conviction. The literature of the New Testament and of the Christian apologists was produced by men who manifested a courage careless of risk to life and fortune rarely seen since Socrates of Athens and Israel's prophets (and others of whom the world was not worthy). When Constantine freed the church, it was in good part because the empire itself was liberalized; but as the Christian creeds were incorporated in the Roman law, freedom of speech declined (so that we largely know what the dissident voices said only from their hostile orthodox critics). While the medieval church both tolerated and even encouraged more freedom of expression than is generally realized, the most notable examples of it are secular: in politics and in higher learning. Without the successful assertion of free speech there would have been no Italian republics; and if the intellectuals, especially in law and philosophy, had not won liberty of teaching, there would have been no universities (within whose walls there was little inhibition of thought)—at least till the fifteenth century. With the Babylonian Captivity and the Schism, freedom is successfully asserted by Conciliarist critics of papal autonomy, but it was lost in the fifteenth century. Then came the age of the Reformation. The destruction of the church's unity has its tragic side, but it was also a momentous event in the history of free speech. Both sides had their notable martyrs: the Thomas Mores and the Thomas Cranmers. The stakes were high: the winning of allegiance on the part of all men from commoners to kings. Mindful of political, economic, social, and other prudential motives, we say that the deeper ones were religious, to which appeals were made in terms untechnical, which any who could read could understand. Theology descended, so to say, from the ivory tower into the marketplace. Publishers of whatever Luther wrote could look forward to guaranteed sales. Any teenager could follow Melanchthon's lectures on theological commonplaces. The Catholic theologian Melchior Cano wrote in the Melanchthonian tradition. And with this we come to Calvin the preacher, commentator, and especially author of the *Institutes*.

Calvin is par excellence the orator of the Reformation era, and the times were made to order for him. His references to the preeminence of the ear over the eye are revealing. He actually used his voice most of the time; he preached several times a week, and much in his commentaries was prepared for class lectures. His audiences represented a general cross-section of society, with no specific preparation for theology through years of drilling in a technical vocabulary, as was usual in a theological faculty at the universities. When he spoke he addressed the whole man: mind, will, feeling. In all this he observed the canons of classical rhetoric. These canons also said that he must expound with clarity (i.e., clarity to the general run of men), with agreeableness (so that he would not put his

35

hearers to sleep), and in such a manner as to move. All this is required for persuasion. The orator does not appeal to the mind alone, as the philosopher does, so as to convince; he intends to persuade for change of faith, or confirmation of faith, and for action. Rhetorical canons also say what kind of proofs to use, which are three in number: logical proof (through enthymeme, the truncated syllogism), ethical proof (the orator as a man must be of one piece, not contradictory in his teaching), pathetic proof (his teaching must be his over-arching passion).

So much for Calvin the speaker. What of him as a writer? The classical literature gave the answer. Its authors wrote so clearly, agreeably, and persuasively, because they wrote with a general cross-section of society in mind. That is what Calvin did.

To say that Calvin spoke and wrote in the sophistic tradition is to say the truth. But to conclude that this means his works are a tissue of sophistry would be wrong. The Greek sophists have been scorned too much, largely because only Plato's opinion of them has been heard. A century ago George Grote (d. 1871) raised his voice against Plato's unfairness. Since then it has more and more become clear that there were some very good sophists, the most distinguished being Isocrates (B.C. 436-338), a contemporary of Plato. It is clear now that the bad sophist uses oratory for unworthy ends, but that the good one aims at accomplishing some good. The bad has really no message; the good has something to say. It was this good sophistic tradition that the early Christian preachers revived, whose sermons were discourses responsive to the rules of rhetorical art: they indeed had something to say that contrasted sharply with much of the empire's second sophistic.

But to put Calvin down as just another sophist—even a very good, nay, even a great one—is not to understand him well. For after all, Isocrates was a schoolman who turned out alumni distinguished for success through good sense, breadth of mind, and mastery of address. His greatest contribution was as inaugurator of what today we call the four-year college. But such we do not associate with Calvin. To assess him as an orator it is more proper to think in terms of Demosthenes, Cicero, and the great Christian preachers of the fourth century of the Christian era (for example, the great Cappadocians). These lived in critical times: Demosthenes when Greece was threatened with loss of political independence by the Macedonians, Cicero when the republic was in mortal danger, the Cappadocians, Basil the Great and Gregory of Nyssa when Christianity might have lost the fruits of Constantine's victory because it lacked vision of a Christian world culture. My effort is not to say that Calvin was as great as these, only that his thrust is comparable. He was certain that, but for the rise of evangelicalism, there was everywhere institutional degeneration and decay. Like the named greats of classical and early Christian times he felt the burden upon him to rethink everything: for Calvin this was aimed at a regeneration of Christianity. This was to be the substance of his message as an orator.

His first step was to join the expanding lay French Movement (largely influenced by Luther and Melanchthon). The decision must have been long in the making. All through the disturbed 1520s he steadily aimed at learning only. Even in his Seneca commentaries (1532) he seems unaware of anything outside the ivory tower. He might then have approved the words of a Cujacius, a top scholar in the history of Roman law, who (perhaps about 1560) was asked why he paid no attention to religious reform. "Does it have anything to do," he asked, "with studies on the Roman procurators?" To change from involvement only with scholarship and scholars to involvement with a nonprofessional lay movement that was fast losing political protection, was a wrench indeed. Upon his conversion, St. Augustine's last temptation to abandon his old life came in a vision of the ladies with whom he never again would have fun. So it could have been with Calvin: would he never again submerge himself in those lovely Latin and Greek classical texts? He must have reassessed his humanism. With all its good, what was it doing toward keeping the world from falling apart! A step by step report of progress toward his decision cannot be made. When at last he made it and joined the movement, precisely then he was reborn as an orator. These people, moved by the German reform but leaderless as sheep having no shepherd, *these* would be his audiences, *these* his reading public.

What this orator had to say would occupy him the rest of his life. But the main categories of his message were likely hit upon quite early. This movement had to be defended, instructed, and organized. Defense came first, expressed in his inspired and eloquent letter to King Francis I (which, by the way, remained in front of every edition of the *Institutes*). Instruction took its most distinguished form in his *Institutes* (the word *institutio* means instruction). Organization, not least though last, was forecast in the *Institutes*, elaborated in his church order. This was for institutional perpetuation, which necessitated a church polity that would be continuously dynamic, responsive to the parish but also to the ecumene.

*   *   *

In conclusion, we may in part summarize, in part make comparisons.

1. Both St. Thomas and Calvin remained whole men while pursuing different methods. Calvin was as rational as St. Thomas, and St. Thomas was a master of persuasive art in his sermons. Both were first-rate scholars. Each according to his situation and light rethought the Christian faith and culture.

2. The church of St. Thomas's era was a self-assured unity, that of Calvin's time was breaking up. Had Calvin lived in the thirteenth century, he might have been moved

to compassion for the alienated Albigensians much as St. Dominic and after him St. Thomas had been, and St. Thomas might have had a like feeling about the alienated brethren of Calvin's time. So, at least, I like to think, considering the spirit of both men.

3. Each method has its hazards. The philosophical disputation becomes speechless at any moment when an objection fails of a proper reply. The essence of disputation, as in all dialectics, is openness, because it pertains to propositions that are probable. There are things necessarily true, but who shall give to even one premise in logic a phrasing that has not been challenged? As to rhetoric, the hazard is not less. Aristotle's rule still holds that the final judge of any speech is the audience.

4. The two methods have been rivals ever since the fifth century B.C. By words rhetoric can protect, instruct, and move to good action the millions. By analysis the philosopher shows whether the words are responsive to the laws of noncontradiction and coherence. The latter addresses the relatively few, and as such is an art of a kind of intellectual elite; the former addresses the many, is therefore an art agreeable to democracies. It is class versus classlessness, patrician versus plebs.

5. Each in its kind has helped make Western civilization dynamic, and each maintaining its own integrity has contributed to the vigor (if also to the tempestuousness) of Christianity. I do not wish for a harmonizing of St. Thomas and Calvin by listing sentences and ideas that suggest identities or analogies here and there. But I could wish very strongly to perceive them in that kind of vision in which Werner Jaeger saw all of Greek literature, namely, that all of it expressed a persistent thrust toward the Greeks' finding clarity on what it means to be human. In like manner, I would put the works of Christian writers in a long perspective in which can be seen the thrust of our faith's history toward clarity on what is the meaning of the man in Christ.

III

JOHN CALVIN: DIRECTOR OF MISSIONS
PHILIP E. HUGHES

Prejudice dies hard; and there are few figures around whom prejudice has accumulated more tenaciously than that of John Calvin. There are still many churchmen today who (though in this much vaunted ecumenical age they ought to know better) use the word "Calvinist" as an ecclesiastical term of abuse or a theological swear-word. We are repeatedly assured that missionary or evangelistic

~~~~~~

Philip Edgcumbe Hughes holds the Th.D. from the Australian College of Theology. The editor of **The Churchman** *and* **Church Men Speak,** *Dr. Hughes has lectured and taught at the University of Bristol, Columbia Theological Seminary, Conwell School of Theology, and Westminster Theological Seminary. In 1963 he represented the Church of England at the World Faith and Order Congress. His publications include several monographs, a commentary on II Corinthians in the New International series,* **The Theology of the English Reformers, But for the Grace of God,** *and translations of P. Marcel's* **The Biblical Doctrine of Infant Baptism** *and* **The Register of the Company of Pastors of Geneva in the Time of Calvin.**

40

activity was entirely incompatible with the character of John Calvin both as a man and as a theologian. The purpose of what follows is to demonstrate the falsity and the injustice of this damning judgment.

With regard to Calvin's personal character, it was for a long time a popular practice of his enemies to blacken his name as one of the most unnatural monsters ever to have been born. Today, however, no self-respecting historian would seek to perpetuate the details of the crude calumnies that have been invented against the person of Calvin. Indeed, the evident sincerity of the desire of Roman Catholic scholars like Hans Küng to arrive at a fair and sympathetic understanding of the Reformers of the sixteenth century is as welcome as it is remarkable; so much so, that, by one of the strangest quirks of history, the fiercest detractors of John Calvin are now to be found among Protestants rather than papists. Their hostility is no less damaging because it is necessarily restricted to the use of sweeping generalizations.

It would not be difficult to draw up a catalogue of slanders against Calvin, but two or three examples from recent publications must suffice. According to the Roman Catholic author Erich Fromm, Luther and Calvin "belonged to the ranks of the greatest haters in history" (*The Fear of Freedom*, p. 80). *The Oxford Dictionary of the Christian Church*, edited by F. L. Cross, speaks of the "vindictiveness" of Calvin and describes him as "the unopposed dictator of Geneva" (1957, p. 220). Roland H. Bainton has written that "if Calvin ever wrote anything in favor of religious liberty, it was a typographical error" (preface to his translation of Castellio's *Concerning Heretics*, 1935, p. 74). That even so admirable a historian as A. G. Dickens has his blind spots is apparent when he says that Calvin "trampled down one opponent after another in his steady march toward the triumphant theocracy of his later years" (*The English Reformer*, 1964, p. 198)—though there is reason to hope that these blind spots of his are

41

being eliminated. It follows axiomatically that one who had such hatred for his fellow men and was guilty of such ruthless tyranny could not possibly have felt the compassion for others characteristic of the missionary-hearted Christian, and could not even have understood, let alone promoted, the gospel of divine love and grace.

As for Calvin's theology, we are all familiar with the scornful rationalization that facilely asserts that his horrible doctrine of divine election makes nonsense of all missionary and evangelistic activity. If certain persons are predestined to be saved, and, by simple arithmetic, the remainder are predestined to be lost, then there is nothing that anyone can do about it; and so "Calvinism" is equated with inaction and unconcern.

There is, however, a very considerable difficulty which these indignant critics of Calvin both as man and as theologian fail to take into account, namely, that he did *not* behave himself in the way that they say he did (see my introduction to the *Register of the Company of Pastors of Geneva in the Time of Calvin*, 1966) and that his theology did *not* have the consequences for him that we are assured it must have had. In this respect at least, Calvin would appear to be a true successor of the Apostle Paul! I suppose no passage in Scripture is more "Calvinistic" (to speak anachronistically) than Romans 9:18—"So then God has mercy upon whomever he wills, and he hardens the heart of whomever he wills"; but it leads on without any embarrassment to the great missionary charter of Romans 10:12-15:

> There is no distinction between Jew and Greek; the same Lord is Lord of all and bestows his riches upon all who call upon him. For, "every one who calls upon the name of the Lord will be saved." But how are men to call upon him in whom they have not believed? And how are they to believe in him of whom they have never heard? And how are they to hear without a preacher? And how can men preach unless they are sent?

Let us consider, then, the facts of the case. In the mid-sixteenth century Geneva was a small city-state of some 20,000 inhabitants. Calvin's return to Geneva in 1541, to lead the work of the Reformation there, was at the insistent invitation of the city's government, confirmed by the acclamation of the populace—and it should not be forgotten that both governors and governed knew by first-hand experience what sort of a man Calvin was, for he had already lived and labored in their midst for some two years (1536 to 1538), and it is evident that they did not think they were inviting a misanthropic tyrant to return to their city. In an essay that expertly and trenchantly "debunks" the Calvin legend Basil Hall of Cambridge has written:

> Those who wish to focus denigration of Calvin, and what he stood for, on his supposed cruelty and dictatorial powers fail to come to grips with two major facts. First, if Calvin was a cruel man how did he attract so many, so varied, and so warmly attached friends and associates who speak of his sensitiveness and his charm? The evidence is plain for all to read in the course of his vast correspondence. Secondly, if Calvin had dictatorial control over Genevan affairs, how is it that the records of Geneva show him plainly to have been the servant of its Council which on many occasions rejected out of hand Calvin's wishes for the religious life of Geneva, and was always master in Genevan affairs? A reading of Calvin's farewell speech to the ministers of Geneva made shortly before he died should resolve doubt upon this point. To call Calvin the "dictator of a theocracy" is, in view of the evidence, mere phrase-making prejudice (*The Churchman*, LXXIII, No. 3, Sept. 1959, 124f.).

There is yet another factor that needs to be weighed, and which, as we shall see, is of particular relevance to the theme of this paper. This is the remarkable phenomenon of the great numbers of persons who fled to Geneva for refuge from the fierce persecutions that raged against adherents of the Reformed faith elsewhere in Europe (and especially in France). Is it likely that all these people over so many years would so eagerly have exchanged one tyranny for another? After all, there were other hospitable cities, without a Calvin, whose gates were open to them and where they could be sure of a welcome. But they chose to go to Geneva. And it was Calvin, the so-called "man-hater," who was their champion; for Calvin's most powerful and persistent opponents in Geneva were not those who were out of sympathy with his theology or with the aims of the Reformation, but the Perrinists, who strongly objected to the opening of their city to this influx of foreigners (bringing with them, as they no doubt did, problems of accommodation, of assimilation, and of competition) and maintained that Geneva should be kept for Genevans. It was thanks to Calvin, as much as to anyone else, that the motives of warm humanitarianism triumphed over those of narrow jingoism.

It is important for us to realize, however, that Calvin's Geneva was something far more than a terminus or *Ultima Thule* for Protestant refugees. So far from being an end in itself, Calvin saw it as being a means to a much more splendid end. It was indeed a haven for hundreds of afflicted fugitives. But it was also a school—"the most perfect school of Christ which has been seen on earth since the days of the apostles," according to the estimate of the great Scottish Reformer John Knox, who himself found refuge and schooling in Geneva. Here able and dedicated men, whose faith had been tested in the fires of persecution, were trained and built up in the doctrine of the gospel at the feet of John Calvin, the supreme teacher of the Reformation.

But, again, Calvin's Geneva was something very much more than a haven and a school. It was not a theological ivory tower that lived to itself and for itself, oblivious of its responsibility in the gospel to the needs of others. Human vessels were equipped and refitted in this haven, not to be status symbols like painted yachts safely moored at a fashionable marina, but that they might launch out into the surrounding ocean of the world's need, bravely facing every storm and peril that awaited them in order to bring the light of Christ's gospel to those who were in the ignorance and darkness from which they themselves had originally come. They were taught in this school in order that they in turn might teach others the truth that had set them free. Thus John Knox returned with the evangelical doctrine to his native Scotland; Englishmen went back to lead the cause in England; Italians to Italy; and Frenchmen (who formed the great bulk of the refugees) to France. Inspired by Calvin's truly ecumenical vision, which penetrated far beyond the horizon of his own environment, Geneva became a dynamic center or nucleus from which the vital missionary energy it generated radiated out into the world beyond.

The extent of this missionary activity may well astonish us. Its cost, in terms of human courage and suffering, was high. Its singleness of purpose in the face of daunting odds is a moving challenge to us today. Indeed, this self-giving, outward-looking attitude is all the more remarkable when we remember that the constant demands and difficulties of the church in Geneva itself might understandably have been used as an excuse by Calvin and his colleagues for inability to give attention to matters further afield.

The figures available to us are far from complete; but even so they are eloquent. They are restricted, in the main, to the few years between 1555 and 1562 when it was felt that the names of those who were sent out from Geneva as missionaries might be recorded (though not advertised) with some degree of safety. The outbreak of the wars of religion in France in 1562, with the consequent intensification of the perils attendant on these activities, made it expedient to resort to the practice of imposing a blackout on the names and destinations of these evangelical envoys. Another expedient dictated by ordinary prudence was the use by many of these men of pseudonyms as they executed their hazardous assignments. Indeed, as I have written, it would be hard to exaggerate the extremely hazardous nature of the assignment undertaken by those who sallied forth from Geneva as missionaries. The unbridled hostility to the Reformation meant that the utmost secrecy had to be observed in sending out these evangelical emissaries. . . . Their lines of infiltration were along perilous paths through the mountains, where they were dependent on friendly cottagers for food and hiding in case of necessity. Nor did the danger end when they arrived at their various destinations, for there too the utmost caution had to be observed lest they should be discovered and apprehended, with all the dire consequences that would be involved. Where a congregation was mustered, services were conducted in a private home behind locked doors or in the shadows of a wooded hillside. There were times when, as much for the sake of the work as for his own safety, it became advisable for a missionary-pastor to leave a place because his activities were becoming suspect and his identity was no longer well concealed (he was becoming, as the Register puts it, *"trop découvert"*) (Introduction to the *Register*, as cited above).

During the period between 1555 and 1562, the *Register of the Company of Pastors* mentions by name 88 men who were sent out from Geneva to different places as bearers of the gospel. In actual fact these represent no more than a fraction of the missions that were undertaken. The incompleteness of the *Register* may be gauged, by way of example, from the consideration that in 1561, which appears to have been the peak year for this missionary activity, the dispatch of only twelve men is recorded, whereas evidence from other sources indicates that in that year alone nearly twelve times that many—no less than 142—ventured forth on their respective missions (see Robert M. Kingdon, *Geneva and the Coming of the Wars of Religion in France, 1555-1563*, 1956, pp. 79ff.). For a church, itself struggling, in a small city-republic, this figure indicates a truly amazing missionary zeal and virility, and a fine unconcern for its own frequently pressing needs.

If the sending forth of preachers had been somewhat sporadic prior to 1555, the eclipse of the Perrinist party in that year enabled Calvin to organize this work in a more systematic manner. The whole of France was a potential mission field into the midst of which Geneva jutted like a little promontory or springboard. Since the great majority of the carefully trained emissaries who were sent out were French-speaking, and indeed came originally from France, they were particularly well fitted to minister the gospel in the towns and cities of France. A recital of the places they went would sound like a lesson in French geography. Thus we find them penetrating to the ancient city of Lyon not far to the west of Geneva; southwards to Aix-en-Provence, Nimes, Montpellier, Villefranche, Toulouse, Nérac, and the province of Béarn; along the Atlantic coast to Bordeaux, La Rochelle and the nearby islands, Nantes, Caen, Dieppe, and the Channel Islands; and in the north to Bourges, Tours, Orléans, Poitiers, Rouen, and Paris; besides a host of smaller places too numerous to mention. There were others who ventured into the rugged Piedmontese valleys of Northern Italy in response to the call for help from the Waldensian remnant who for so long had been manfully battling for their very survival.

But the venture that most stirs the imagination was the dispatch of two men across the Atlantic to Brazil. The Register for 1556 simply says, in typically laconic fashion, that on Tuesday 25 August Pierre Richier and Guillaume Charretier were elected to minister in the islands recently conquered by France off the coast of Brazil, and "were subsequently commended to the care of the Lord and sent off with a letter" from the Genevan church. Through the influence of the Huguenot leader, Admiral Coligny, arrangements were made for a group of Protestant emigrants to join the expedition that was being sent out, with the expectation that they would be able to establish a colony in South America and, free from persecution, develop their own culture and at the same time instruct the heathen natives in the gospel of Christ. Richier and Charretier accompanied them in the dual capacity of chaplains to the French Protestants and missionaries to the South Ameri-

47

can Indians. Regrettably, however, the project was ill-fated. Villegagnon, the governor of the expedition, betrayed Coligny's trust in him. He turned against the Calvinists in his party, throwing four of them to a watery grave in the sea because of the faith they confessed, and causing the rest to seek safety by returning to their homeland, which, ironically, they had left in order to enjoy freedom to express and practice their faith without being hated and hunted like animals. Abortive though this project was, it testified strikingly to the far-reaching vision Calvin and his colleagues in Geneva had of their missionary task.

The perilous nature of the missionary enterprises which were organized from Geneva is well illustrated in the *Register*—though perhaps one should add that the *Register* is anything but a martyrology and very frequently information has to be culled from other sources in order to complete the stories of the persons and events which it mentions. On 12 October 1553, some three years prior to the Brazilian interlude, a letter was sent from the Company of Pastors of Geneva to "the believers of certain islands in France," giving them advice for which they had asked and sending them a man (who also carried this letter) to minister in their midst. No names of persons or places are mentioned: the times were too perilous, and the interception of a letter containing names could lead to the direst consequences. It is true that the letter is signed "Charles d'Espeville in the name both of himself and of his brethren"; but this gave away nothing, for "Charles d'Espeville" was a cover-name used on occasions by Calvin when it would have been imprudent for him to sign his real name.

> Most dear brethren [the letter reads], we praise God that He has given you, in your captivity, the desire to serve Him faithfully, so that you are more afraid of being deprived of His grace than of exposing yourselves to the dangers into which the malice of men may bring you. For the brother who bears this letter has told us that you have requested him to return to

you as soon as possible, and that you wish by every means to advance in blessing and to be confirmed in the faith of the Gospel.

They are admonished to be diligent in meeting together for worship and instruction and to separate themselves from the idolatry and superstition of the Roman Church. In due course, when they have proved themselves in these respects and a proper order has been established, but only then, would they be well advised to commence the administration of the sacraments. "It is not lawful," they are told, "for a man to administer the sacraments to you unless you are recognizably a flock of Jesus Christ and a churchly form is found among you." The letter closes in a manner not only typical of such letters from Geneva, but also revealing of the true depth of compassion of Calvin's heart:

> Meanwhile take courage and dedicate yourselves wholeheartedly to God who has purchased you through His own Son at such cost, and surrender both body and soul to Him, showing that you hold His glory more precious than all that this world has to offer. May you value the eternal salvation which is prepared for you in heaven more than this fleeting life. Therefore, and in conclusion, most dear brethren, we shall pray the good Lord to complete what He has begun in you, to advance you in all spiritual blessings, and to keep you under His holy protection.

The persons to whom this letter was addressed were living on the islands off the coast of Saintonge, near La Rochelle (Ile d'Oléron, Ile de Ré, etc.), and the bearer of the letter, who became their first pastor, was Philibert Hamelin. This man prosecuted his ministry with faithfulness until he suffered martyrdom in 1557.

On 27 June 1555 a letter arrived at Geneva from three men, Jean Vernou, Antoine Laborier, and Jean Trigalet, who had set out a week earlier to minister in the Piedmontese valleys, conveying the news that they had got no further than Chambéry, where they had been seized and imprisoned. They in turn were comforted and encouraged by letters from Calvin and his fellow-pastors in Geneva. The text of a subsequent letter from the imprisoned missionaries, dated 1 August 1555, is given in the *Register*. In it they bemoan, not what has befallen them personally, but their "fault," as they now believed it to be, in having sought to protect the evangelical groups to whom they were being sent by dissembling before their interrogators.

Gentlemen and most dear brethren [they write], we have been greatly comforted by the letters which you have kindly written us, especially in seeing by them that your customary magnanimity has supported us despite our fault, which cannot be described as small, as its effects show us all too clearly. Have we achieved anything by what we have done? Have we, by our misguided prudence, prevented what we feared from happening? Alas, no. For three or four days later, when we were still sorrowing over our fault, the news came that Satan was inflicting his fury on those whom we wished to preserve. Our grief was then redoubled; and we knew very well that this was for our humiliation, having learnt that the prudence of men cannot prevent the providence of God. We have in ourselves more than enough imperfections to keep us lowly before God; but this one is so obvious that it exceeds all the others. The Lord God has caused us to feel this most vividly so that for the rest of our lives we may be humbled by it; yet He is willing to pardon us, as we believe He has already done. We entreat you to pray God for us, since the need for prayer is greater than ever—and not so much for us as for these poor people, that God may withdraw His rod from them or may soften them, and that, if it is necessary, He may soon send upon us what He pleases. Meanwhile we shall pray for you and for them while awaiting the outcome of our case, whatever it may be that God is pleased to give us, confident that in guarding our faith, as is our duty, He will enable us to fulfil our calling.

They were, in fact, never released, but were martyred in that same place. The mission to Piedmont was not allowed to fail, however; for, as the *Register* shows, others took their place and, braving all dangers, went forth from Geneva as Christ's ambassadors to these needy parts.

Perhaps no assignment was more hazardous than being sent to minister in Paris, for the enemies of the Reformation in France's capital city were so numerous and influential that to associate oneself with the evangelical cause, however secretly, was tantamount to taking one's life in one's hands. This is amply borne out by the experience of Calvin's trusted lieutenant, Nicolas des Gallars, himself a Frenchman of aristocratic family, on one such expedition. Des Gallars set out from Geneva on 16 August 1557, accompanied by the envoy who had come from Paris to request the dispatch of a minister to strengthen the cause there. On the way this companion was captured and put to death, but des Gallars managed to escape and continued on to his destination. But a still greater misfortune awaited him there. On 7 September he sent a letter to Geneva conveying the news that three days previously their congregation had suffered a disastrous raid. "Almost two hundred persons are held captive by the enemy," he wrote, "who threaten them with all kinds of dire consequences. Among them are many distinguished individuals, both men and women; but not the least respect is shown either for their family or for their station." This was the notorious affair of the Rue Saint-Jacques, which was to have international repercussions. Calvin replied immediately. "Although my first reaction was one of horror," he wrote, "and I was almost prostrated with grief, yet I lost no time in seeking a means of remedy"—and he outlines, though under the circumstances in cryptic terms, the steps that had been taken to influence the situation in Paris for the better. Calvin also tells des Gallars that his wife was with him and that he had taken care to keep the worst news from her, lest she should be overanxious. In this we have a glimpse of Calvin's thoughtfulness and solicitude for others. His letter concludes with the following words: "May the Lord guide you and them [des Gallars' colleagues in

51

Paris] in this crisis by the spirit of wisdom, understanding, and uprightness; may He be present with you and with the cover of His wings protect, strengthen, and sustain both you and the whole church!"

Finally, there is a noteworthy letter received in Geneva on 15 July 1552. It is true that the letter came from five young men who were not missionaries but students, and that they had been studying in Lausanne (where Beza was then teaching) not Geneva (the academy there was not founded by Calvin until 1558). But these young men were missionaries in the making, and their letter is addressed to "our brothers of the church of Geneva." On returning to their native land, they were seized and thrown into prison in Lyon; and there they were put to death because of the faith they professed stedfastly to the end. It is a most moving document, and these five young martyrs speak clearly across the centuries, eloquently attesting to the fact that, at its deepest level, training for the Christian ministry consists of something more than the accumulation of learning and the passing of exams.

> Very dear brothers in our Lord Jesus Christ [they write], since you have been informed of our captivity and of the fury which drives our enemies to persecute and afflict us, we felt it would be good to let you know of the liberty of our spirit and of the wonderful assistance and consolation which our good Father and Savior gives us in these dark prison cells, so that you may participate not only in our affliction of which you have heard but also in our consolation, as members of the same body who all participate in common both in the good and in the evil which comes to pass. For this reason we want you to know that, although our body is confined here between two walls, yet our spirit has never been so free and so comforted, and has never previously contemplated so fully and so vividly as now the great heavenly riches and treasures and the truth of the promises which God has made to His children; so much so, that we seem not only to believe and hope in them but even to see them with our eyes and touch them with our hands, so great and remarkable is the assistance of our God in our bonds and imprisonment. So far, indeed, are we from wishing to

regard our affliction as a curse of God, as the world and the flesh wish to regard it, that we regard it rather as the greatest blessing that has ever come upon us; for in it we are made true children of God, brothers and companions of Jesus Christ, the Son of God, and are conformed to His image; and by it the possession of our eternal inheritance is confirmed to us. Further, we are bold to say and affirm that we shall derive more profit in this school for our salvation than has ever been the case in any place where we have studied; and we testify that this is the true school of the children of God in which they learn more than the disciples of the philosophers ever did in their universities—indeed, that it must not be imagined that one can have a true understanding of many of the passages of Scripture without having been instructed by the Teacher of all truth in this college. It is true enough that one can have some knowledge of Scripture and can talk about it and discuss it a great deal; but this is like playing at charades. We therefore praise God with all our heart and give Him undying thanks that He has been pleased to give us by His grace not only the theory of His Word but also the practice of it, and that He has granted us this honor—which is no small thing for vessels so poor and fragile and mere worms creeping on the earth—by bringing us out before men to be His witnesses and giving us constancy to confess His name and maintain the truth of His holy Word before those who are unwilling to hear it, indeed who persecute it with all their force—to us, we say, who previously were afraid to confess it even to a poor ignorant laborer who would have heard it eagerly. We pray you most affectionately to thank our good God with us for granting us so great a blessing, so that many may return thanks to Him, beseeching Him that, as He has commenced this work in us, so He will complete it, to the end that all glory may be given to Him, and that, whether we live or die, all may be to His honor and glory, to the edification of His poor Church, and to the advancement of our salvation. Amen!

Though great numbers of people today know little or nothing about this school of affliction there are many in the world today who are being trained in it. Let us not forget that we are one with them in Christ and that it is our duty and privilege to uphold them by our prayers and our communications. We need to learn afresh today—and this is a lesson that the Geneva of John Calvin can teach us—that the church of Christ is not merely a haven of comfort and security nor a religious club where Christians may take their ease (though too many regard it as such), but a dynamic fellowship of the reborn, empowered by the Holy Spirit, and commissioned to penetrate into all the world with the liberating message of God's free grace in Christ Jesus.

IV

THE GENEVAN MISSION TO BRAZIL

R. PIERCE BEAVER

The continuing Protestant world mission began in the seventeenth century with the evangelization of the American Indians by the New England Puritans supported by their English brethren, and with the work of conversion in the Orient undertaken by the chaplains of the Dutch East

R. Pierce Beaver received his doctorate of philosophy from Cornell University in 1933. He has served as a pastor in the Evangelical and Reformed Church, as a missionary to China, as director of the Missionary Research Library in New York City, as secretary of the division of Foreign Missions of the National Council of Churches, as member of the editorial boards of **Church History** *and* **Journal of Church and State.** *He has lectured and taught at Union Seminary (New York), Central China Union Theological Seminary, the Theological Seminary of the Evangelical and Reformed Church, the Biblical Seminary of New York, and at the divinity school of the University of Chicago. He is the author of* **House of God, Envoys of Peace, Ecumenical Beginnings: The History of Comity, All Loves Excelling,** *and* **The Missionary Between the Times.**

55

Indies Company. These were both enterprises of Calvinists. Early in the eighteenth century German pietism in the form of the Danish-Halle Mission and Moravian missions added a second force. At the end of that century the great modern missionary movement began with Calvinists again taking the initiative. Until well into the nineteenth century the primary motivation for the missionary movement out of Britain, the Netherlands, and the American churches was the giving of glory to God and compassion for perishing souls and for the wretched social condition of men. These motives were derived from Calvinist theology.

Much has been made by historians of a lack of missionary concern on the part of Luther, Calvin, and their fellow Reformers. It is often said that there is only one basis for mission in Calvin's teaching, namely, the duty of Christian magistrates to introduce the true religion to all subjects (cf. *Inst.* IV,xx,9). That would make mission a function of imperialism and colonialism. However, while Calvin may not have explicitly exhorted the Reformed churches to undertake mission, he certainly was not hostile to worldwide evangelism. In fact, his theology logically calls for mission action, although he did not enunciate it.

Passages widely scattered throughout Calvin's commentaries strongly support the idea of mission. For example, Calvin declares that "there is no people and no rank in the world that is excluded from salvation; because God wishes that the gospel should be proclaimed to all without exception. Now the preaching of the gospel gives life; and hence . . . God invites all equally to partake of salvation" (*Comm.* I Tim. 2:4). Christ is Lord as well as Savior of all. He states further that Christ is not sent to the Jews only, that he may reign over them, but that he may hold his sway over the whole earth" (*Comm.* Isa. 2:4). The church is gathered indiscriminately out of all nations. God's Kingdom extends its boundaries far and wide, and the task of the church in the extension of it is far from finished. "The Kingdom of Christ was only begun in the world, when God commanded the gospel to be everywhere proclaimed, and ... at this day its course is not as yet complete" (*Comm.* Mic. 2:1-4). If all this is true, then some form of mission seems to be required for that universal proclamation of the gospel and extension of the Kingdom.

Moreover, Calvin's view of the apostolic office was not such as to make mission impossible, even though he held it to be extraordinary and not part of the regular order of settled churches. He writes in the *Institutes*: "The 'apostles,' therefore, were missionaries, who were to reduce the world from their revolt to true obedience to God, and to establish his Kingdom universally by the proclaiming of the gospel" (IV,iii,4). They were "appointed to lay the foundations of the Church all over the world." Evangelists perform similar functions, but were inferior to the apostles in dignity. Although these offices were not instituted for perpetual continuance and have no place in "well-constituted churches," nevertheless, Calvin writes: "I do not deny, that, even since that period, God has sometimes raised up apostles or evangelists in their stead, as he has done in our own time." The church of Geneva actually sent out a company of evangelists, if not apostles, apparently with the approbation of Calvin. It can be inferred that the mission had his support, since it would never have been dispatched if he had not given approval. Had this mission succeeded, circumstances would then have forced the great theologian to deal explicitly and systematically with mission, and not leave it to his spiritual descendants some generations later to find and respond to the implicit motivation in his teaching.

The mission was sent in connection with an attempt to establish a French colony in Brazil and at the request of its founder. Pope Alexander VI in 1493 divided the world by a north-south line drawn one hundred leagues west of the Azores, and gave to the Spanish crown the exclusive right to conquest and trade in all lands not inhabited and ruled by Christians west of that line and to the Portuguese crown the same rights to the east. The line was shifted to 370 leagues west of the Azores the next year by the Treaty of Tordesillas, and in 1506 Pope Julius II reaffirmed the donation of his predecessor. It was to the surprise of all that Brazil was discovered jutting east of that line, and so fell to Portugal. The Protestant powers of northern Europe did not recognize the right of the Pope so to dispose of most of the globe, nor did His Most Catholic Majesty, the King of France. France, therefore, carved out for herself a wilderness empire in Canada and the Mississippi Valley and dared to contend with Spain and Portugal in the Caribbean and South America. Portugal's main interests were in establishing a trade monopoly with India and the East, and consequently her holdings in Brazil expanded rather slowly. French vessels from Brittany and Normandy, encountering relatively little interference from the Portuguese men-of-war, regularly visited the coast, especially the area about the Bay of Rio de Janeiro, and brought home cargoes of brazilwood, from which a highly prized red dye was made. Hearing accounts of this country from Breton sea-captains, Villegagnon chose it as the site of a colony which was to be the first in a region that would be known as France Antartique.

It is not easy to determine the character of Villegagnon since his Huguenot antagonists ascribed to him a villainous character and hypocrisy, and even Marc Lescarbot in his *History of New France* (1609) is contemptuous of the man who failed to effect a permanent settlement. It is claimed that his real intention was to establish a kingdom for himself in America, but there is no ground for that view. Nicolas Durand was born about 1510 at Provins in Champagne, son of a lawyer who in 1516 got the title sieur de Villegagnon. Nicolas was a fellow student of John Calvin at Paris, but their paths parted when Villegagnon took the profession of arms. He became a Knight of Malta, and was cited for bravery during the campaign of Charles V against Algiers. He fought briefly in Hungary against the Turks and in the campaign for Piedmont. Then he turned to a naval career. During a naval expedition aiding the Scots he circumnavigated Scotland, and then, escaping the pursuing English fleet, carried Mary Queen of Scots and her entourage safely to France. He next fought in defense of Malta and published an account of the siege. The Knight was appointed vice admiral of Brittany, but, having lost a quarrel with the governor of Brest over fortifications of that port, determined to undertake a colonial expedition to Brazil.[1]

The vice admiral of Brittany sought the aid of the Grand Admiral of France, Gaspard de Coligny, in support of his venture. Coligny had not yet announced his adherence to the Reformed Church, but his interest in and protection of the Huguenots was known. Lescarbot states:

> Inasmuch as such an enterprise could not well be carried out without the recognition, co-operation, consent, and authority of the Lord Admiral, who at that time was Gaspard de Coligny, a man imbued with the ideas of the so-called Reformed religion, he gave the said Lord Admiral, and also several noblemen and others of the so-called Reform, to understand, whether hypocritically or no, that he had long had not only an extreme desire to betake himself to some far-off land where he could freely and sincerely serve God in accordance with the purity of the Gospel; but also that he desired to establish there for all who wished to retire a refuge from persecution, which was, in fact, at that time so violent against the Protestants that several of both sexes and of divers ranks throughout the whole kingdom of France had been burned alive, and their goods confiscated, by edicts of the King and by decisions of the High Court of Parliament.[2]

Coligny was evidently impressed with both the mercantile possibility of such a colony and the opportunity of an establishment where Protestants could at least share religious liberty with Roman Catholics. The admiral was in high favor with the court, and through his intervention Henry II authorized the expedition and granted three ships

59

and 10,000 livres for expenses. When few volunteers could be found for a settlement in a place supposed to be inhabited by cannibals, the king also gave permission to recruit among the inmates of the prisons of the realm. Well-known Huguenots did join the expedition, including the sieurs de la Chapelle and de Boissi and the navigator Nicolas Barré, who wrote the account of the voyage incorporated by Lescarbot into his *History*. The ex-monk, André Thevet, who made maps of the region and drawings of the inhabitants, was also a member.

The little fleet sailed from Havre de Grace on July 16, 1555, and reached Guanabara or Rio de Janeiro on November 10. Villegagnon chose a small barren island devoid of water as the site of settlement because of its apparent ease of defense. Later a cistern was built to store rain water. Here a defense work was built and named Fort Coligny. Relations with the neighboring Tupinamba Indians were good, since the French brazilwood traders had been on excellent terms with them and the newcomers were welcomed as allies against the Portuguese. Foodstuffs were imported from the mainland. But the colonists did not like the strange starchy "root" that was the staple diet, abhorred the strict regime imposed, resented heavy labor on the fortifications, were irked by the total lack of female companionship, and rebelled against the strict segregation from the Indians that prevented contact with native women. A mutiny occurred, was severely repressed, and the ringleader executed.

It was evident to the commandant that he needed reinforcements of a better quality. Whatever his original intentions may have been, Villegagnon now turned to the Huguenots with determination. When his ships sailed for France at the beginning of February 1556, they carried his appeals to Coligny and to the church of Geneva. His letter is not preserved in either the correspondence of Calvin or the archives of the canton. (There exists only a brief summary of the affairs of the Company of Pastors for this period, since the secretary was then mortally ill.) Jean de Léry, whose life was to be profoundly affected by this letter, gives its contents. The letter asked that the church of Geneva immediately send to Villegagnon ministers of the Word of God and with them numerous other persons "well instructed in the Christian religion" in order better to reform him and his people and "to bring the savages to the knowledge of their salvation."[3] Thus the question of mission was set squarely before the church of Geneva. "Upon receiving these letters and hearing this news," de Léry states, "the church of Geneva at once gave thanks to God for the extension of the reign of Jesus Christ in a country so distant and likewise so foreign and among a nation entirely without knowledge of the true God." The response was positive.

Villegagnon's letter to the church was supported by another from Admiral Coligny to his former neighbor now resident at Bossy near Geneva, Philippe de Corguilleray, sieur du Pont, requesting him to lead the party. The church and ministers added their plea, and Corguilleray du Pont accepted, although rather old and infirm for such an arduous undertaking. He is described as a man of indomitable faith and great strength of character. Most of the recruits were refugees, some not yet officially admitted to residence in Geneva. The ministers chosen were Pierre Richier, spiritual superior of the company, then aged fifty, a former Discalced (barefoot) Carmelite, a doctor of theology, and Guillaume Chartier, aged thirty. Villegagnon had particularly asked for artisans. Among the eleven lay recruits were four carpenters or cabinetmakers, a leather worker, a cutler, and a tailor. Thevet calls Jean de Léry a shoemaker, and he may have learned that trade when very young, but, still a youth, he was in Geneva as a student of theology. Another of the party, Jean Gardien, probably made the engravings that illustrate Léry's book.

It is to Jean de Léry that we are indebted for a detailed account of this mission and extensive observations on the

Tupinambas, the topography, the fauna, and the flora of the region. His journal, under the title *Histoire d'un voyage fait en la terre de Brésil,* was published in Geneva in 1578 as an answer to misrepresentations in André Thevet's *La cosmographie universelle* of 1578.[4] In 1564 he had written for Jean Crespin an account of the martyrs of Fort Coligny.[5] After his return from Brazil Léry was ordained and became a noted minister in the Reformed Church. He lived through the famous siege of Sancerre in 1573 and published a narrative of the horrors of that event.

Calvin had gone to Frankfurt at this time, but he was kept informed of everything of importance that was happening at Geneva and gave his advice. There is no doubt that he was consulted about the mission, because the leaders carried letters from him to Villegagnon (cf. Letter 2612, *C.R.*, XLIV,438f.). There is extant a letter from Pastor Nicolas des Gallars, dated September 16, reporting to Calvin that Richier, Chartier, and du Pont had departed from Geneva "full of ardor" on the 8th of that month (Letter 2530, *C.R.*, XLIV,278f.). The party visited Admiral Coligny at his home at Châtillon-sur-Loing. Richier, writing to Calvin, calls him "the conductor and chief (*dux et caput*) of our enterprise" (Letter 2613, *C.R.*, XLIV,441). After a short sojourn in Paris they arrived at the port of Honfleur, where they were joined by a large company of Huguenots recruited through the efforts of Coligny. The whole personnel, including the sailors, numbered 300. Among them were a woman in charge of five young girls destined to be married to colonists already on the ground and six young boys who were expected to live with the Tupinambas, learn their language, and serve as interpreters. They embarked in three ships under command of a nephew of Villegagnon, Bois-le-Compte. After many adventures the little fleet arrived at Guanabara on March 7, 1557, and disembarked at Fort Coligny on the 10th.

When they had given thanks to God for a safe journey,

the new arrivals proceeded to the waiting commandant. He received them joyfully, embracing the leaders, and loudly thanking God that his long-standing desire had been fulfilled. Corguilleray du Pont and the pastors announced that they had come expressly, in accord with his letters to Geneva, to found in that country a Reformed Church in conformity to the word of God alone.[6] Villegagnon thereupon publicly declared that this was to be a land where the persecuted faithful in France, Spain, or anywhere might serve God in purity according to his will. He said that he wanted to be a father to them. A service of thanksgiving followed.

In the days soon after the coming of the reinforcements community discipline and worship under the commandant's magistracy became much like that at Geneva, although Villegagnon bore down hard on the newcomers, making them labor diligently on building the fortifications. Pastor Richier declared that they had found a "new St. Paul" in the governor.[7] The Lord's supper was celebrated by the Geneva rite on March 21 and Villegagnon was the first to receive communion. Léry reproduces in full the commandant's public prayers on that occasion. Letters of Richier, Chartier, and Villegagnon himself to Calvin all attest the joy, serenity, and optimism that prevailed (cf. Letters 2609, 2612, 2613, *C.R.*, XLIV,434-43).

First acquaintance with the Indians discouraged the pastors' hope of converting them. Villegagnon described them to Calvin as "devoid of all courtesy and humanity," "living without religion, honor, or virtue," "beasts bearing the human figure" (Letter 2612). Pastor Richier's first report to John Calvin was much the same (Letter 2609). He wrote that the savages were characterized by unimaginable barbarism. They were cannibals, crassly stupid, incapable of distinguishing good from evil. What other peoples hold to be vices, these considered virtues. They were scarcely to be distinguished from beasts. Above all, they had no idea of the existence of God. They did not obey his law nor recognize his power and bounty. "The result is," Richier wrote, "we are frustrated in our hope of revealing Christ to them." It might be thought that their minds were *tabula rasa* on which it would be easy to paint, but the tremendous obstacle of the language barrier was made all the more insurmountable by the absence of interpreters faithful to our Lord.

One month was a rather short period of time in which to come to such definite conclusions. But however discouraging the prospect, the Genevese were not prepared to abandon the mission. Richier told Calvin that they would try to advance that enterprise by stages and wait patiently for the boys who had been placed with the Indians to grow up among them and master the language in such a natural manner. He terminates the passage thus: "Since where the Most High has given us this task, we expect this Edom to become a future possession for Christ." Meanwhile he would put his hope in the anticipated increase of pious and industrious Reformed Church members who by conversation and example would impress the Tupinambas.

Jean de Léry was not lightheartedly and unreflectively optimistic about the prospects of conversion, but unlike the senior pastor he saw ground for hope within a reasonable period of endeavor. He did not make up his mind about Indian society at first glance, but carefully observed the Tupinambas through the whole course of his residence among them, visiting their villages, even staying with them on occasion. He made careful notes on their rites and customs, on their beliefs and attitudes as revealed in conversations. These pioneer anthropological field notes have been written up in the descriptive second part of his book, the section called "Brazil in 1557." He does not gloss over customs and practices repulsive to Europeans, but neither does he condemn these people for being different. War and the fate of prisoners are horrible, and he graphically describes them. Cannibal feasting, which he has witnessed, is execrable, but civilized Christian Europeans can be rela-

64

tively more cruel and sometimes resort to the same practice in times of famine. The excessive dress and ornamentation of French women may actually cause more wickedness than the nudity of primitive women. He found the Tupinambas to be without knowledge of the only true God and his creation of the world. Indeed, they were without any intimation of divinity. They knew only evil spirits which oppressed them, and against whom they sought the aid of sorcerers called Caräibes. He learned much about their practices and observed their major ceremony. Nevertheless, in his estimation these people had some good traits. They were, for example, hospitable to friend and stranger. As unpromising as these Tupinambas might appear to Frenchmen, "nevertheless," Léry affirms, "it is my opinion that if Villegagnon had not turned against the Reformed religion, and if we had been able to remain in that country for a longer time, we would have drawn and won over some of them to Christ" (p. 343).

Léry was most informal in his evangelistic approach to the Indians. He took advantage of opportunities that arose naturally in the friendly intercourse between them. Thus on one occasion when he and some other Frenchmen were with the Tupinambas and the tribesmen were politely watching them dine, an old man was curious about the meaning of prayer at the beginning and end of their meal. Why did the French all take off their hats twice and remain silent while one of them spoke? Did he address someone present or absent, or did he talk to himself? Léry says "we" seized this occasion to speak to them about the true religion. Given the original dual intention of the mission, it would not be rash to assume that most of the Genevan laymen, if not the larger company of Huguenots, would be ready to try to teach the gospel to the natives. At least the theological student associates others with him in the beginning of this encounter. Then he himself launched into a discourse which lasted two hours, during which the assembly listened intently. He began with a declaration of the unseen God who knows the inmost heart of every man, told of creation, and recounted God's providence right down to his bringing the French safely over the seas. Believers in this God need not fear Aygnan, the chief of evil spirits, either in this life or the other. He assured his hearers that if they would turn from their errors, abandon dependence on the Caraïbes, renounce their barbarism, and no longer eat their enemies, they would become as blessed as the French. Discussion followed the talk. The Indians were so moved that they earnestly promised to follow this teaching and never again eat human flesh. They knelt with the French for prayers, which the interpreter explained. But before Léry and his companions fell asleep, many warriors began dancing around a fire, chanting war songs, and telling absent enemies that they would eat them raw! "A good example of corrupt human nature," Léry remarked.

The writer adds a second example to show how, had there been enough time, the Brazilian natives could easily have been brought to the knowledge of God. While seeking provisions on the mainland Léry chanced to meet two Tupinambas and an Oneanen, who with his wife had been visiting friends and was returning to his own country. As they walked through the forest with its beautiful plants and great trees, amid beautiful fragrant flowers and flocks of birds singing joyously, the young man burst into song, praising God for all this beauty and glory in the words of Psalm 104. When the song ended, the Oneanen remarked that Léry had sung marvelously well, and that they had listened with joy, but they wished to know what the words meant. There was no other Frenchman with him, and the student tried his best to explain in the Tupinamba language. He told them about the Creator of all the world of nature, and that this song, given by the Spirit of God, had first been sung by a great prophet ten thousand moons ago. The four hearers listened attentively, now and then uttering a grunt of interest. They exclaimed about the happiness of white men who knew such secrets kept from such poor beings as themselves. In parting they presented Léry with their pet aguti. He adds the reflection that although these Americans may be barbarous and cruel with their enemies, they actually discourse better than most European peasants and reason better than folk who think themselves clever.

On the first occasion reported, the Indians related to Léry a tradition that many, many moons ago—so long a time that when it was could not be known—a white stranger had visited that land and told their ancestors that very same teaching about the true God. This raised for Léry the question whether this might have been one of the twelve apostles. The theory was then current in Europe that the apostles had preached to all peoples throughout the world, and in the early seventeenth century this was made the basis of rejection of missions. The view got its classical expression in the famous decision of the theological faculty of Wittenberg in 1651. That pronouncement set forth authoritatively the view evidently already widely held in Léry's time that the Great Commission had been addressed by Christ solely to the twelve apostles as their personal privilege and duty, that they had actually preached the gospel throughout the whole earth, that the binding character of the commandment ceased when the last of them died, and that, if any people anywhere had heard and not believed, they were justly damned and their fate was of no concern to the church.[8] Léry was skeptical of noncanonical *acts* of various apostles and other early works that related fabulous tales of apostolic travel and preaching. However, Paul's words in Romans 10:18, quoted from Psalm 19, referred, according to numerous commentators, to the apostles: "Their sound went out into all the earth, and their words unto the end of the world." It might be that one or more of the apostles had actually visited this land of savages, and if that were true the savages would be less excusable in the last day. Nevertheless, they alone were not responsible for their present ignorance of God and true religion, and the churches of Europe were not devoid of responsibility.[9] Putting his observations together with biblical texts, the theological student came to the conclusion that the American Indians were descendants of Cain, who, expelled from the land of Canaan by the Hebrews, had crossed the seas and settled on this continent. This in Léry's mind confirmed all the more the truth of Scripture. So clearly accepting the missionary responsibility of Christians, it weighed heavily on Jean de Léry that no conversions were made during the time the Genevan band was in Brazil.

It was the extreme shortness of time that thwarted the hope of converting the Indians, according to both Pastor Richier and Léry. Had the second aim of the venture succeeded and a permanent Huguenot refuge been established, there would have been opportunity to persist in evangelism. Large reinforcements were expected, and Villegagnon had charged Nicolas Carmeau, who sailed as his courier on the *Rosée* on April 1, to bring over from France a large number of men, women, and children, stating that he would pay the expenses of the Reformed.[10] However, that second goal was also unachieved, because Villegagnon soon changed face. He had informed Calvin that his letter had been read in council and inscribed in the register as a permanent guide for the colony (Letter 2612, *C.R.*, XLIV, 440). He had the ministers preach twice on Sunday and once each day. The young women were married to colonists by Protestant rites. However, the celebration of the Lord's supper, despite that first show of unity, brought conflict. Its instigator was a certain Jean Cointac, whose marriage to one of the girls had been the third of those ceremonies performed. He had been a student at the Sorbonne, but it is not clear whether he had been ordained. He claimed that Villegagnon had promised to make him bishop of the colony. Before the first celebration of the Lord's supper, when examined by the ministers, he had renounced the papacy and had given satisfactory answers on all points. Now he lodged a complaint against the pastors and challenged their doctrines and practices. He cited the church fathers in support of his arguments. Villegagnon sided with Cointac and supported transubstantiation and other doctrines. It was agreed to submit the disputed points to Calvin, whom Villegagnon then called one of the wisest men since the apostles and one of the best and purest expounders of Holy Scripture. Guillaume Chartier was sent to Geneva to bring back Calvin's answers.

By the time of the Pentecost celebration of the eucharist in June, Villegagnon, egged on by Cointac, was prescribing the order of service, and demanding the admixture of water with wine and other points. When reminded that he had agreed to accept Calvin's decisions on these matters he vehemently denounced the theologian of Geneva as a heretic. Léry reports that the commandant had received letters from the Cardinal of Loraine and others admonishing him to renounce his support of the Calvinist heresy. Villegagnon grew daily more despotic and erratic. The colonists could tell from the color of his splendid garments what his mood was on any particular day.

Finally, exasperated beyond further endurance, the Genevese through their spokesman, Corguilleray du Pont, informed Villegagnon that since he had rejected the gospel they were no longer his subjects, would not remain in his service, and henceforth would not carry earth and stones for the fortifications.

Attempting to starve the group into submission, the commandant cut off their rations. Not only the Genevese suffered from his displeasure and consequent despotic and cruel behavior. He crushed a conspiracy by having the leaders thrown into the sea. Léry and some others who visited the Indians for two weeks were put in irons, but du Pont got them released. Some of the Huguenots proposed to throw Villegagnon himself into the sea and feed him to the fish, but respect for Admiral Coligny restrained them. At length finding it impossible to break the resolution of the Geneva band, who were getting food by trading with the Indians, the governor at the end of October ordered them off the island. They considered going into refuge among more distant Indians but feared that they might not be as friendly as the Tupinambas. The only alternative was to join other colonists who had left the island and settled about a mile and a half away on the bank of the Guanabara River at a place which they called La Briqueterie. This situation gave Léry and some others opportunity to get better acquainted with the Tupinambas. The sieurs de la Chapelle and de Boissi were expelled also for their stand on the gospel and joined the Genevese. Here they remained for two months living on fish and the products of the country.

A small ship, *Le Jacques*, scouting for another site for a Huguenot refuge colony, arrived and took on a cargo of brazilwood. Passage for fifteen was arranged. Villegagnon did not oppose their departure, but he wrote secret instructions, to be given to the first judge to whom the indictment might be delivered, to execute the Genevese as traitors and heretics. Fortunately, the document actually fell into the hands of officials friendly to the Reformed cause, and it was later used against its author.

The ship sailed on January 4, 1558. It ran into heavy seas after making only twenty leagues along the coast and began to founder. After some anxious hours five of the Calvinists agreed to return to land and were given a boat. They had a difficult experience but eventually made their way back to Fort Coligny. The *Jacques* had a most perilous voyage. The passengers and crew were reduced to eating leather and rats, and reached Nantes more dead than alive. Léry's journal graphically describes the ordeal of that voyage. At Nantes they met with great kindness and were treated by skilled physicians.

The fate of the five men who returned to Fort Coligny,

as related later to Jean de Léry by eyewitnesses, was narrated by him in the document which he wrote for Jean Crespin for inclusion in the *Histoire des Martyrs*. These men were Jean du Bordel, Mathieu Vermeuil, Pierre Bourdon, André Lafon, and Jean Le Balleur. Villegagnon received them with seeming kindness and restored them to status in the community on condition that they not attempt to win anyone to the Reformed position. However, the commandant soon accused them of being spies and proceeded to do away with three of them. He spared André Lafon and Jean Le Balleur, he said later, because they did not appear "so dangerous" and he wanted to keep them in his service.[11] Lafon was a tailor and essential to the maintenance of Villegagnon's vanity. The other was useful as a cutler. The men were arrested and required to answer certain points of doctrine and subscribe their names within twelve hours. The eldest, Jean Bordel, drew up their confession of faith, which is still extant.[12] He, Bourdon, Vermeuil, and Lafon signed their names to it. The men were on the mainland and might have escaped, but conscience demanded that they meet this test of their faith. The commandant on February 9 ordered them brought before him in the Fort. Bourdon was too ill to move. The others refused to recant their confession. They were thrown into prison overnight. The next morning, after they had again refused to retract, Villegagnon ordered first Bordel, and then Vermeuil, cast into the sea from a high rock. Later that day the governor crossed to the mainland and confronted Bourdon, who was too sick to rise. The commandant ordered him to be bound, strangled, and thrown into the ocean. Thus the end of the Genevan mission was the martyrdom of three of its members whose heroic witness was to inspire and strengthen the Reformed people in France and Switzerland.

Not long after this Villegagnon returned to France and tried to enter into controversy with Geneva. He attempted to engage Calvin himself,[13] but it is reported that Calvin trod his letter under foot. Others did contend with him. Charges and countercharges flew back and forth (Letter 3229, *C.R.*, XLVI,149-151). Until the end of his days he fought Calvinists and Lutherans with his pen. His leg was shattered by a cannonball during the siege of Rouen in 1562. He became the ambassador of the Knights of Malta to the court of France in 1568, and died at Beauvais on January 9, 1571. Antarctic France had vanished in the meantime. The Portuguese viceroy of San Vincente, Mem de Sa, early in 1560 sent an expedition of twenty-two ships and two thousand men to attack Fort Coligny. When this force struck on February 21, most of the colonists were on the mainland under Bois-le-Compte, Villegagnon's nephew and lieutenant. The garrison held out until March 15 when it surrendered, only to be massacred. The Frenchmen who had escaped into the interior were mostly killed by Indians. A few were eventually rescued by a French ship homeward bound from China.

Reformed churches venerate the martyrs of Brazil. The short-lived mission had no statistical fruits in conversions. Yet it has historical importance. Confronted with a challenge to undertake mission, the church of Geneva responded immediately. The circumstantial evidence points to Calvin's approbation. There was no hostility to either the concept or practice of mission. The Swiss had no colonies to direct Geneva soon again to the heathen in far places. The French government fostered only Roman Catholic missions in its colonial territories, and after a short period of toleration the Reformed Church was bitterly persecuted. Historical circumstances would next present the challenge to the Calvinists of Holland and New England, and they would respond positively both theologically and practically.

NOTES

1. Thomas E. V. Smith, "Villegaignon," *Papers of the American Society of Church History*, III, 1891, 185-206. There are two biographies as well: Arthur

Heulhard, *Villegagnon, Roi d'Amerique* (Paris, 1897); and T. Alves Nogueira, *Der Mönchsritter Villegagnon* (Leipzig, 1887).

2. Marc Lescarbot, *History of New France* (tr. by W. L. Grant) (Toronto, 1907), I, 148.

3. Jean de Léry, *Journal de Bord de Jean de Léry en la Terre de Brésil 1557, presénté et commenté par M.-R. Mayeux* (Paris, 1957), p. 51; Lescarbot, p. 157; Calvin, *Correspondence*, Letter 2613, *Corpus Reformatorum*, XLIV, 442.

4. Latin version, *Historia Navigationis in Brasiliam*, Geneva: Eusctache Vignon, 1586; the 1957 edition (see note 3) is the principal source for this essay and is the one cited and quoted. Léry, supported by Lescarbot, can be assumed to be the authority unless otherwise indicated. Thevet's *La cosmographie universelle* (1575), vol. II (the pertinent part) was published in Paris in 1875 and 1953, but has not been seen. A recent treatment of the mission with extensive quotations from Léry is Oliver Reverdin, *Quatorze Calvinistes chez les Topinambous* (Geneva, 1957). A short essay on the mission is Gonzalo Baez-Camargo, "The Earliest Protestant Missionary Venture in Latin America," *Church History*, XXI, No. 2, June 1952, 135-145.

5. Found in Crespin, *Histoire des martyrs persécutés et mis à mort pour la vérité de l'Evangile* ... (Geneva, 1619).

6. Léry, p. 104.

7. Léry, p. 107; Lescarbot, p. 179.

8. Gustav Warneck, *Outline of a History of Protestant Missions* (tr. from the 7th German ed. by George Robson) (New York, 1901), pp. 27-28.

9. Léry, p. 344.

10. Léry, p. 117.

11. Villegagnon, *Propositiones Contentienses*, p. 13, quoted by Reverdin, p. 59.

12. Crespin, II, 510-13.

13. See Reverdin, p. 108, and Smith, pp. 200-204.

V

WHAT CALVIN LEARNED AT STRASSBURG

FRANKLIN H. LITTELL

We live in a time of rapid change. One of the marks of the age is a radical reshuffling of alignments and alliances among the churches. There was a time not long ago when any genuine traffic between Catholics and Protestants was strictly clandestine, regarded in both camps as a kind of ultimate disloyalty. Now most topics of concern are open-

Franklin H. Littell received the Ph.D. from Yale in 1946. He has served as minister of youth at Central Methodist Church in Detroit, dean of the Boston University chapel, president of Iowa Wesleyan University, and professor at Emory University, Perkins School of Theology, Chicago Theological Seminary, and Temple University. He has been a consultant to the National Conference on Christians and Jews, and president of Christians Concerned for Israel. He has contributed articles to **Reformation Studies**, *and has written several books, including* **The Anabaptist View of the Church, The Free Church, The German Phoenix: A Tribute to Menno Simons**, *and* **Sermons for Intellectuals.**

ly discussed, and Catholics and Protestants even celebrate communion together on occasion.

Similarly, among Protestant groups great change is evident. A man's worst adversaries are sometimes those of his own household, whereas in the congregations of erstwhile opponents he finds allies to go forth with him to cast out demons and heal the distressed. The relationship of those who stand in the tradition of Calvin's theocracy and those who claim spiritual descent from the Anabaptists is very much like that today.

A few years ago the two groups were still debating the "church type" and the "sect type" and arguing the measure of Christian responsibility in the conduct of government. Today there is a perception that the issues lie elsewhere. In the churches, they lie between a radical individualism and the renewal of Christian community. In the body politic, major areas of life—public education, social welfare, higher education, medical care—have been largely freed from church control or influence altogether. All Christians share a like restlessness, a feeling of being shoved to the margins of historical and national development. Whether this unease is firmly grounded or not, the descendants of both Calvin and the Anabaptists can surely agree that their chief problem is no longer with each other. A sketch of one period of the early and common history of the two groups, when encounter proved fruitful in spite of many obstacles, may indicate that both already owe each other much and that neither needs to feel any real embarrassment if the mutual indebtedness increases in the years ahead.

*   *   *

To take one example, the covenant theology of the Calvinist Reformers took firm shape in a lively exchange with the Anabaptists. It is a serious mistake, though an ancient one, to identify the *Täufer* as individualists or enthusiasts (*Schwärmer*). Such charges will no longer stand the best of historical evidence, as the distinguished scholar Leonard Verduin has made quite clear in *The Reformers and Their Stepchildren*. The Anabaptists were champions of religious liberty and the voluntary covenant, and they consciously separated from and condemned the revolutionaries and the spiritualizers.[1]

The first church covenant on record was adopted by an Anabaptist congregation in Frankfurt am Main. Michael Satteer's *Seven Articles* of 1527 were concluded in a covenant to do God's will, sealed by baptism of believers into the "body of Christ."[2] For the Anabaptists the "door into the sheep-stall" was adult baptism, and the covenant concept spread with the movement into Strassburg, Hesse, and the Netherlands. In a short time the writing of names in a book came to be practiced, referring to the angel's writing in the Book of Life.

One misses the real point of controversy if he erroneously assumes that the Anabaptists were individualists or defenders of private inspiration. On the contrary, they were critics of Christendom and defenders of the voluntary covenant. Even here it would be a mistake to accuse them of synergistic tendencies, much less Pelagian. This was the error of the famous Lutheran scholar Karl Holl, who assumed that because the Anabaptists advocated voluntary church affiliation *vis-à-vis* the government they must also be theological voluntarists. Holl used the term *Freiwilligkeitskirche* to elide the political and theological issues,[3] which tells us more about his view of church-state relations than it does of the actual Anabaptist position. It is perfectly possible to have a strong view of the independence of the church from political control (voluntary-ism) without having a theologically questionable stance (voluntarism). In point of fact, the general Anabaptist view anticipated that later articulated by Richard Baxter and John Wesley, although Pilgram Marpeck—for example—was a hardline Augustinian.

The distinguished Swiss Reformed scholar Gottlob Schrenk has shown how the idea of the covenant came to the fore in the debates of the sixteenth-century Reformed churchmen with the Anabaptists. The Anabaptists called themselves comrades of the covenant (*Bundesgenossen*) and referred to baptism as a covenant (*puntnus*). Schrenk summarized the results of the encounter between Anabaptists and Reformed leaders as follows:

> Zwingli is for Reformed theology the original renewer of the biblical view of the covenant, but the demand for it admittedly came to him from the Anabaptist side.... The battle with the Anabaptists and the determination to maintain the *Volkskirche* are the driving forces which stand behind this view.[4]

The conflict between Anabaptists and Reformed leaders was far more interesting than any ascribed conflict of individualists and churchmen. The Reformed churchmen, in line with their determination to effect a reformation of whole territories, accented the covenant of fathers and sons, the importance of continuity and tradition. The Anabaptists, in line with their radical break from the whole idea of "sacral" civilization ("Christendom"), accented the importance of the covenant of a good conscience toward God—among those present and accounted for.

Zwingli stressed the covenant with Adam, renewed in clearer terms with Noah and Abraham. There is only one covenant from the beginning to the end of the world: Abraham is saved in Christ, as we are. Thus infant baptism is like circumcision, and the children of Christians are secured in the covenant and the passover even as those of Israel of old.[5] For Heinrich Bullinger, the identity of the covenant is even plainer: the differences are in the "accidents," not the substance of the matter. For Calvin—especially as he expounded it in the 1559 edition of the *Institutes*—there is a single covenant of grace, different only in the *modus administrationis*. Others followed him:

77

Musculus, Ursinus, Olevianus. It was not until the time of the federal theologian and social reformer Johann the Elder (younger brother of William of Orange), of Herborn, that a quite different separation of covenants becomes normative—to be completed in the social and political philosophies of Althusius and Coccejus. With them, we can perceive the beginnings of an utterly voluntary church discipline on the one hand, and a political covenant pointing toward popular sovereignty and "secular" government on the other.

But before that happened there were conflicts and encounters of both negative and constitutive significance to both parties: the Anabaptists, pioneer free churchmen, and the Reformed churchmen, sometimes defenders of Calvinist state churches and the reluctant fathers of popular sovereignty and constitutional liberty.

*   *   *

For those who love religious liberty, the Landgrave Philipp of Hesse was—until his granddaughter's husband, William of Orange, became *Stadholder* in the Lowlands—the most winsome political figure of sixteenth-century Europe. It was Philipp whose troops, wearing the same colors as those of Duke John of Saxony at Speyer in 1526, stayed the emperor's intention forcibly to suppress the evangelical cause. It was Philipp who cooperated with the Archbishop of Mainz to defeat Franz von Sickingen and the revolt of the knights, and later pacified the peasants and joined with Bishop Franz von Waldeck to suppress the Münsterite revolt (1534-35). It was Philipp who cooperated with his friend Ulrich Zwingli to try to bring the evangelical parties together in a mighty alliance reaching from Zurich to Denmark[6]—a plan largely wrecked by Martin Luther following the Marburg Colloquy (1529). To Philipp alone is due the saving of Württemberg from the Habsburgs and for the Reformation.[7] Above all, it was

Philipp who, inspired by a vision of the New Testament and early church, encouraged his preachers to attempt to effect a genuinely apostolic reformation in *Land Hessen*.

Among the results of Philipp's churchly leadership was the founding of the first Protestant university in the world, at Marburg, as recommended by a church synod brought together at his instigation in 1526.[8] Another result was a policy of toleration, indeed reconciliation, which led him to embrace the truce of the Interim in spite of members of his own family, and to urge in his last will and testament that his sons work for a reunion of Protestantism and Roman Catholicism.

The measure by which he judged the matter of persecution or toleration was "not the Scripture, but the practice of the ancient church, which stood near the time of Christ and thereby best knew His opinion and that of the apostles."[9]

Another result of his churchmanship was that Hesse became, after the Ziegenhain Synod of 1539, the only *Landeskirche* with a formal structure of church discipline.[10] And, although even official *Kirchenpfleger* were unable to maintain a pattern of discipline within the established church of Hesse, the *Gemeinschaften* (fellowships modeled on the early church) gave a noteworthy quality of ethical and moral earnestness.[11] This whole policy of church discipline, which resulted from the 1538 Disputation of Butzer and the Anabaptist elders at Marburg, was fixed with Philipp's express encouragement. Although the consequences in Hesse were chiefly seen in the pacification of the Anabaptists, the ramifications for the liturgy and church order came to be felt as far away as England and Geneva. Both confirmation and church discipline, in Protestantism, derive to a large degree from the discussions and debates carried on by Martin Butzer with Philipp of Hesse's express encouragement, and the peculiar style of the reformation in Hesse was profoundly shaped by the

Landgrave's conviction that the true church is that which follows the model of Christ and the apostles.

*   *   *

The period of special reference is precisely the time of exile in Strassburg (1538-41), between Calvin's periods of leadership at Geneva.

There is no particular point here in discussing the general mutualities and conflicts between Calvin and the Wittenbergers, the Anabaptists (whom he never rightly knew), the followers of Zwingli and Bullinger (who were incorporated into the general Reformed camp with Calvinism in 1549), and Butzer and his associates. The question is whether presumptive evidence may be found for the conclusion that during his exile in Strassburg Calvin learned certain lessons of lasting significance for his thought and for the life of those churches he chiefly influenced.

The indebtedness of the Reformed churches to the Anabaptists in connection with the church covenant has been discussed. Let us now consider two other churchly practices that came to the fore during this period, both of considerable importance to the life of the Reformed churches: confirmation and church discipline.

During the Middle Ages there had been a churchly rite known as *Firmunge*, which occurred at approximately the time of transition from childhood to maturity—a kind of Christian puberty rite, as it were. Evangelical confirmation, with specific catechetical instruction and public profession of faith, was instituted as a result of public debates between the Strassburg Reformers and representatives of the "Left Wing of the Reformation." The South German Brethren, under the leadership of the lay theologian Pilgram Marpeck, were the wing of the Anabaptist movement most committed to covenant theology.[12] By them it was linked to believers' baptism. In the debate with Butzer that

preceded his expulsion from the city, Marpeck charged
that the city preachers had not

> preached freely under the Cross of Christ, but under the
> protection of the princes and cities. Therefore it is not to be
> wondered that the Word of God brought no fruit. To this day
> there is no Christian order in Strassburg.[13]

Those who came after him, including spiritualizers like
Casper Schwenckfeld and Johannes Bünderlin, disagreed
with Marpeck's strong insistence that the covenant of the
Free Church was grounded in rigorous church discipline.
But they too criticized the city preachers for accepting the
baptized into full membership without training or personal
decision.

In a public disputation of June 10-14, 1533, Schwenckfeld finally charged the city preachers that, if they would
not desist from infant baptism, they should at least provide a "Ceremonie" at which young people, upon coming
of age, could make public profession of the faith.[14] This
proposal apparently took root, for the next year Martin
Butzer advanced a plan for evangelical confirmation in his
Ad Monasterienses. From there the rite spread to Zurich,
Wittenberg, and other Protestant centers, and was written
by Butzer into the 1551 *Book of Common Prayer*.

For Butzer, confirmation was related to the larger question of church discipline.[15] This too he learned in disputation with the Anabaptists.[16] Although the Strassburg city
council refused to accept it, a plan of church discipline was
incorporated into the church order of Hesse. The circumstances that led up to this action of the Ziegenhain Synod
(1529) are remarkable.

In his confession of faith at Strassburg, Pilgram Marpeck
had, like other Anabaptists, insisted that matters of faith
ought to be governed solely by the Spirit of Christ in his
church: no government had any authority over the *po-
testas Christi:*

81

> When the outward magistrate is allowed to rule in the Kingdom of Christ, then it is blasphemy against the Holy Spirit, the (true) Lord and ruler without human assistance.[17]

Philipp too felt that persecution was contrary to the standard of the early church, where differences had been handled by brotherly admonition, prayer, and dialogue. Rather than put the separatists (*Täufer*) to death, he pointed out the difference between them and the Münster revolutionaries, and insisted that none of his subjects be put to death for matters of faith. Only insurrectionists should be reduced by the sword. He called upon Butzer to engage Peter Tesch and other imprisoned Anabaptist elders in disputation, and himself attended many of the sessions. The result was that Hesse became the only land, Protestant or Catholic, in which the Anabaptists were reclaimed in considerable number to the established church.[18]

The Anabaptists claimed in the disputation that they had separated from the public services of the church of the land because no true apostolic discipline ("the Ban") was maintained; if there is a grievance, it must be taken to the church (Matthew 18:17). After considerable further exchange and the presentation of a confession of faith by the imprisoned, which was recognized to be orthodox, the Reformers of Hesse agreed to reinstitute church discipline, and the Anabaptists agreed to return to the public worship of God. Butzer informed Philipp that he felt the Anabaptists were right in criticizing the absence of church discipline, and Philipp ordered that the preachers be brought together in synod to institute such on the New Testament model. At Ziegenhain the responsibility for church discipline was separated from direct control by the civil power,[19] although the eldership was made an office of both congregation and town council.

The consequences of the settlement were far reaching, even though in Hesse the plan to use energetically both the *censura* and the ban was never carried out very effectively.

Butzer returned to Strassburg from his striking success at winning the Anabaptists back to the Protestant established order, and we may be sure that Calvin—his friend and sometime house guest—received the report at its most glowing.

*　　*　　*

Calvin was most reluctant to return to the misery of leading the faction-torn city of Geneva, and he did so only under strongest pressure from its representatives and his associates. Above all, he was compelled by his sense of the strategic importance of the gateway city to the cause of the gospel in France and Italy.

He agreed to go back only when the *Ordonnances ecclesiastiques* were provisionally agreed to, and these rules were presented to the first sitting of the city council (September 13, 1541) after his return. As is clearly indicated in the 1559 edition of the *Institutes*, Calvin was less concerned for the liberty of a Christian man than for the honor of God and the integrity of the true community of the faithful. Church discipline, expanded in detail and significance, came to be called the "third mark" (*tertior nota*) of the church—along with the word and sacramental life.

With Calvin's return, we have the beginning of the theocracy. Initially, the distinction between religious and socio-political concerns was recognized: the Venerable Company had charge of the preachers, and the consistory—made up of the preachers and twelve laymen—had charge of moral life and discipline. In effect, however, the often precarious political situation, the wars of religion and the threat of Roman Catholic power resurgent with the Council of Trent, and the attempted rebellion of the "libertines" erased the distinction in practical effect. In 1542-46, there were 58 hangings and 76 expulsions from the city (population about 20,000), and during a 1545 plague 34 women were burned or quartered as witches. Geneva, which functioned as a bastion of Protestant reform in dangerous territory, sacrificed religious liberty to international policy.

In Hesse church discipline remained a dead letter for the sake of a comprehensive church policy. In Geneva it was enforced by expelling dissenters. The Christianization of the city, and the use of the city as a base for international church politics—even as later in New England's standing order, erased for the time any religious liberty or practical distinction between the religious and the political covenant. As in the fortress of the high Middle Ages, "heresy" became treason and treason heresy.

Nevertheless, there was implicit in Calvin and Calvinism an awareness that discipline is, finally, a matter of the integrity of the church. In those other geographical areas where the logic of minority status worked itself out, for example, among the radical Puritans and in the religious pluralism of the Germanies, the double covenant was openly recognized. In a strictly voluntary situation such as the United States today, we may turn to the Calvin who learned from Butzer at Strassburg, rather than to the Calvin who was complicit in Servetus' burning, to find inspiration and style for the dialogue.

*   *   *

In the fulness of time, the priesthood of all believers that both Butzer and Calvin affirmed, which led them to accept the use of the ban as part of the essential equipment of the *ecclesia militans*, has produced a people in the churches who will not obey decisions they have had no part in making. Through loyally maintained covenants, however—thoroughly studied and "talked up"—they are in many places today resisting the blandishments of the new gnostic cults and mounting a new breakthrough in Christian mission and ministry.

In the process of resisting false ideologies and harnessing an effective witness, the spiritual descendants of Pilgram Marpeck, Martin Butzer, and John Calvin are again meeting in dialogue. This time, assigned a new task in a new situation, they find themselves more allies than adversaries. They have—to prejudge the terms of their coming cooperation—common enemies in totalitarianism and secularism, and a common Lord in him who is able to use the most unlikely instruments to effect his purposes and fulfil his promises to mankind. In the present battles, the Calvinists and the Anabaptists are not only learning to admit their mutual indebtedness: they are learning to call each other brother in Christ.

NOTES

1. Franklin H. Littell, *The Origins of Sectarian Protestantism* (New York, 1964), pp. 21f., 106.

2. Champlin Burrage, *The Church Covenant Idea* (Philadelphia, 1904), pp. 15f.

3. Karl Holl, *Gesammelte Aufsätze zur Kirchengeschichte* (Tübingen, 6th edition, 1932), I, 428-29.

4. Gottlob Schrenk, *Gottesreich und Bund im älteren Protestantismus* (Gütersloh, 1923), p. 36.

5. Schrenk, p. 39.

6. W. Lenz, "Zwingli und Landgraf Philipp," *Briegers Zeitschrift für Kirchengeschichte,* III (1879), 46-47.

7. Herbert Grundmann, *Landgraf Philipp von Hessen auf dem Augsburger Reichstag 1530* (Gütersloh, 1959).

8. Ernst Benz, "Die Gründung der Universität Marburg und die Reformation," 54 *Pastoralblatt für Kurhessen-Waldeck* (1952), 5:7-19.

9. Fritz Hermann, *Das Interim in Hessen* (Marburg, 1901), p. 213.

10. Heinrich Bornkamm, *Martin Bucers Bedeutung für die europäische Reformationsgeschichte* (Gütersloh, 1952), p. 15.

11. G. J. van de Poll, *Martin Bucer's Liturgical Ideas* (Assen, 1954), p. 65.

12. John C. Wenger, "The Theology of Pilgram Marpeck," *The Mennonite Quarterly Review,* XII (1938), 4:208.

13. J. Loserth, "Zwei biographische Skizzen aus der Zeit der Widertäufer in Tirol," *Zeitschrift des Ferdinandeums für Tirol und Vorarlberg,* XI (1895), III:39:282.

14. See "Konfirmation," in Christian Hege and Christian Neff (eds.), *Mennonitisches Lexikon* (Frankfurt, 1913–), II, 533-36.

15. Martin Butzer, *Résumé Sommaire de la Doctrine Chrétienne* (Paris, 1951), pp. 52, 62.

16. Franklin H. Littell, "New Light on Butzer's Significance," in *Reformation Studies* (Richmond, Virginia, 1962), pp. 144-67.

17. Pilgram Marpeck, "Confession of Faith Composed at Strassburg (December, 1531-January, 1532)," transcribed and edited by John C. Wenger, *The Mennonite Quarterly Review*, XII (1938), 3:197.

18. Franklin H. Littell, *Landgraf Philipp und die Toleranz* (Bad Nauheim, 1957), pp. 33f.

19. Jacques Courvoisier, *La Notion d'Église chez Bucer* (Paris, 1933), chapter IV.

VI

THE INTENT OF THE CALVINISTIC LITURGY

JAMES H. NICHOLS

There is some insight to be gained from the pursuit of the literary development of the Reformed services, and their classification into those of a mass structure on the one hand, and those of the preaching and communion orders on the other. But it is striking to observe the convergence of the two types of structure in actual practice. The mass originally developed, after all, out of some-

James H. Nichols was awarded a Ph.D. by Yale University in 1941, and has received honorary degrees from Franklin and Marshall College and Monmouth College. He has been professor at Macalester College, the University of Chicago, the Chicago Divinity School, and Princeton Theological Seminary. He was editor of the **Journal of Presbyterian History** *and* **The Mercersburg Theology,** *and co-editor of* **Church History.** *His articles have appeared in* **The Challenge of Our Culture** *and* **Religion in America.** *Among his various books are* **Primer for Protestants, Evanston: An Interpretation, History of Christianity 1650-1950,** *and* **Corporate Worship in the Reformed Tradition.**

thing very like the conjunction of a preaching service with a communion order. And a eucharistic service with sermon but without communion was not very different from a preaching service. Nor did the Reformed leaders of the sixteenth century seem to take much interest in literary structure in this way. They accepted and approved of diversity in such matters. They were much more interested in the content and meaning of sermons and sacraments and how these were related to the nurture and witness of the church. We might do well to examine their worship more nearly according to their own perspectives. For this the Butzer-Calvin service probably supplies the most representative order, and has the added advantage of some interpretation from Calvin's writing.

With a confidence emulated by some, though not all, contemporary biblical scholars, Calvin appealed to the "invariable custom" of the early church. "No meeting of the church should take place," he asserted, "without the Word, prayers, partaking of the Supper, and almsgiving" (*Inst.* IV,xvii,44). This list of essential elements may serve us as a convenient outline for discussing the meaning of the Butzer-Calvin service.

* * *

First of all Calvin requires the preaching of the word. And this was probably the most striking emphasis of the Reformers generally. Whatever else it was, the Reformation was a great preaching revival, probably the greatest in the history of the Christian church. All the Reformers preached prodigiously. In most of the Reformed communities there were two or three sermons on the Lord's day and several during the week, sometimes daily. The appetite for the word preached was startling by modern standards, both in the length and solidity of sermons and in the number of them desired by the congregations. Perhaps it is only intelligible against the general and nearly complete late medieval neglect of the word. For the twelve thousand people of Geneva there were fifteen services with sermon every week, distributed through three parishes. And although many or most modern historians refer to the length of these sermons as wearisome, they rarely supply contemporary judgments to this effect. Such comments are usually more revealing of the historian and his method than of his documents.

The word, in Reformation usage, meant the written word and the preached word as conveying the Incarnate Word. The great preaching revival went hand in hand with the rediscovery of the Bible and its general accessibility in the new translations, as of Luther, Tyndale, Le Fèvre and Olivetan. Men entered with amazement and wonder into the world of the Bible, known for generations to the layman only in scattered quotations and snippets. The preached word was closely identified with Scripture, so that in the services of the Reformed churches the Scripture reading and sermon are ordinarily referred to in one comprehensive rubric—"the word." It was one liturgical act to read the Scripture and to preach it. The sermon followed immediately on the reading, and was not separated from it (as in many modern services) by anthems, prayers, and other elements. The reading and preaching were introduced by a prayer to the Holy Spirit to quicken this word in the lives of the congregation, and, in Calvin's custom, often followed again by a bidding prayer catching up some of the themes.

It was because the sermon was so intimately related to the Scripture that it was possible to restore the unity of preaching, communion, and prayers without the seams showing. If the sermon is not so related to the Scripture, it becomes an interruption of the liturgy—or, more likely, one has a religious or moral oration surrounded by opening and closing exercises. But the Reformed preacher was expected to do faithful expository preaching, to present to his congregation the promise of God as found in his text.

89

There were two alternative systems of arranging the readings over the year. The North German Lutherans and Anglicans used the medieval biblical anthology and its calendar. The South German Lutherans and the rest of the Reformed returned to the patristic custom and the model of such preachers as Augustine and Chrysostom. A series of sermons on John, Isaiah, Job, Deuteronomy would be better able to set forth the biblical message in its own proportions and movement, they felt, than sermons based on someone's selections for an anthology. Such series would be interrupted, of course, for the half-dozen major festivals of the church year.

Reformation preaching was characteristically expository preaching, and also what has been more recently called "kerygmatic" preaching. Its substance, that is, was the kerygma or proclamation of the apostles as to what God had done and would do in Christ Jesus. The gospel had originally been not a book, as Luther pointed out, but sermons, testimonies of apostolic faith. Such living witness communicates the word more effectively than merely reading the Bible, even today. It is the function of the preacher to make us Christ's contemporaries, so that his redeeming deeds and dying become our present righteousness. The apostles and those who continue the apostolic preaching are God's messengers by whom his revelation is conveyed to man. God does not ordinarily use angels, private revelations, or even private reading of Scripture.

The preacher of the word is thus God's instrument in a terrifyingly direct way. "I am certain," said Luther, "that when I enter the pulpit to preach or stand at the lectern to read, it is not my word, but my tongue is the pen of a ready writer." Preaching the word is revelation in the same way that the Scripture is revelation. All that one could say about God's declaration and disclosure of himself in Scripture is also true of his word preached. The preacher is to expound the promise of Scripture in the worshipping congregation in the expectancy that God will use his words, will act through him to condemn and forgive, to regenerate and cleanse, to console and fortify. Similarly we are to hear the word preached as though he were near to us, face to face.

In recent years when such expectations are not usual, Forsyth has accustomed us again to the idea of preaching as "sacramental." For Luther there is but one sacrament, God manifesting his mercy to us in Christ Jesus, which he does through the three sacramental "signs" of baptism, the preaching of forgiveness, and the Lord's supper. So for Calvin the preacher's words are "signs" through which Christ approaches men and effects his kingly rule in the world, creating and upholding his church. God's greatest gift to the church is the preaching of the good news that is mighty to save, alive with blessing and judgment. The preacher of grace is performing the most important act any man can accomplish in this life. The fruitful hearing of the word is the greatest blessing any of us will know in this life. And the church is most church when the word is preached and heard, for there God is actually calling, justifying, sanctifying his people.

The Anabaptists did not have this very high view of the sacramental nature of the word preached. There were those who held that the Spirit is given directly to the soul, apart from the word, and that the preaching of Christ is frequently inefficacious. Calvin is slightly more cautious than Luther in identifying the sacramental acts of the church simply as God's acts. God the Spirit, Calvin teaches, works both in the word preached and in the hearer to enable its recognition. But the gospel is never preached in vain.

The central and constituting function of the Christian ministry was thus the preaching of the redeeming word. Those who did not so preach were outside the apostolic succession, and not true priests. Most sixteenth-century priests and bishops were in this category. They did not and could not preach that word which should be heard whenever the church of God assembled.

To preserve the consensus of the preachers several Reformed communities utilized a kind of preachers' workshop. This practice began in Zurich in 1525, and it was called prophesying (a reference to Paul's advice in I Cor. 14:29-33: "Let two or three prophets speak"). In Zurich the preachers of the city gathered in the cathedral five days a week for their school of the prophets. A selected passage was examined in Latin, Hebrew, or Greek. Then its use in a sermon was discussed and a sermon finally preached on it. The Zurich translation of the Bible was largely hammered out in this way.

A similar practice was followed once a week in à Lasco's Church of the Strangers in London and in the English refugee congregation in Geneva. Here all members of the congregation were encouraged to present questions to the ministers through a committee. In Elizabethan England ministers gathered in certain counties at a central church and engaged in exposition, one after another, of a selected passage. Questions from the congregation were also entertained. These "prophesyings" were suppressed by the queen as potential presbyteries, but in one form or another the practice was widespread as a discipline in biblical preaching and a guardian of doctrinal agreement.

*   *   *

The second element in every meeting of the church is the prayers. These are of two types, said Calvin—spoken and sung. We must say something of each.

It is significant that Calvin discusses church music under the rubric "common prayer." He had a high opinion of the place of music in worship. The sung portions of the Calvinist service, in fact, are most of what is in the strict sense "liturgical," that is, the congregational part in worship.

Aulcuns Pseaumes (1539), was printed. Six months after he left, an edition of the Psalms with prayers was printed in 160 pages, the parent of the line of Reformed service books.

Marot followed Calvin to Geneva and there completed versions of a number of Psalms before he died. Beza finished them, and by 1562 the Huguenot psalter was complete. Musically this psalter owes most to Louis Bourgeois. Douen estimates that about thirty of the tunes were borrowed from Strassburg and some thirty-two more were adaptations of identifiable secular songs, often simply developments of an initial phrase. The conception was like that of plain chant: a simple melodic line, a note to each syllable, designed to be sung in unison without accompaniment. But the metrical rhythm gave a new dynamic to the familiar tonality and made it easier to master. The tunes illustrate the transition from the medieval tones to modern major and minor keys. Of the 125 tones, Douen classifies 52 as Gregorian, 38 as in major key, and 35 as close to our minor.

The success of this collection was enormous. Today it is hard to imagine the effect of fresh and excellent verse translations set to eminently singable, clear, simple melodies. It was in this way that the Bible first came home to every layman, and the success of these metrical psalters was comparable to that of the Bible translations. Dathenus translated the French psalter into Dutch (1566) and Lobwasser into German (1573); and in both of these languages it had even wider circulation than in the original. It swept Europe and became the most powerful proselyting instrument of the Reformed tradition. Even strict Lutherans with their unrivalled hymnody spoke with some irritation and envy of "*le sirene Calviniste.*"

Calvin's views on the place of music in worship are stated in his prefaces to the 1542 and 1545 editions. He assessed music as the first gift—or one of the first gifts—of God for man's recreation. "It has power to enter the heart

95

like wine poured into a vessel, with good or evil effect." In worship, in particular, it "has great force and vigor to move and inflame the hearts of men to invoke and praise God with a more vehement and ardent zeal." But in worship the musical or aesthetic interest must not be permitted to outweigh the devotional. The music is to carry the text, but not to distract attention from its meaning. And since the congregation is itself to sing and not to be displaced by trained musicians, the musical form must be held down to the capacities of general congregations. Calvin resisted the desire of the musicians to make the sung liturgy more interesting. When Goudimel published his arrangements for four voices (1565), the preface states explicitly that these settings are not for church use but for singing in homes. Where the harmonized versions became popular, of course, they *did* work their way back into church worship. The metrical Psalms became the staple of family and private worship as well as of the Lord's day liturgy, and soon many knew the psalter by heart. And as for the congregation, a Dutch visitor to Strassburg three or four years after Calvin had left found that the singing of the French liturgy moved him to tears of joy.

Part of the appeal of the Psalms was that the language was that of the inspired Scriptures, and presented Christ and his benefits, so to speak, in God's own language. Some such feeling seems at least to have inhibited for generations the development of a Reformed hymnody.

In the *Pseaumes de David* of 1562 each Psalm is prefaced by a sentence or two facilitating such interpretation. For example, the second Psalm is captioned: "Here we see how David and his kingdom form a true image and sure prophecy of Jesus Christ and his reign." And the book was furnished with an index of two pages, for the use of the church and of individuals, with which one might find the Psalm appropriate to various kinds of events.

If thine enemies cluster against thee, and go about with

96

their bloody hand to destroy thee, go not thou about by mans help to revenge it, for al mens judgments are not trustie, but require God to be judge, for he alone is judge, and say the 26, 35, 43 psalmes.

If they press more fiercelie on thee, although they be in numbers like an armed hoast, fear them not which thus reject thee, as though thou wert not annointed and elect by God, but sing the 27 psalme (Scholes, 270f., from Hawkin's).

In some editions of the Huguenot and Scottish psalters a full set of 150 collects, one for each Psalm, is found. Since the Psalms were scheduled systematically, this yielded, in effect, another type of "collect for the day." Thus, on Psalm 69 was set forth the following (in the Scots dialect):

Eternall Father, and God of all consolatioun, that for the satisfactioun of our sinnes, wald cast down thy onelie Sonne to extreame dolours and anguishes, and hes ordayned thy Kirk to pas be the samin way of affliction:

We beseik the maist effecteouslie, that forsamekill as we are destitute of all help of men, we may sa mekill the mair be assurit of thy mercie and gudenes, that we may praise the sam before all creatures, baith now and euer mair. So be it.

The Reformed sense of the church as the "people of God," a holy nation, was particularly close, of course, to the Hebraic view of an elect people. The Reformers also shared a very direct and vivid sense of God's providential direction of human history. The outcome of battle and the incidence of disease were at once read religiously, as signs of warning or mercy from the Lord of history. The imagination of the sixteenth century was not yet intrigued by "secondary causes" and had not yet become subdued to mechanical and impersonal analogies for the processes of nature. The Reformed Church rather viewed nature, as does the Psalmist, as manifestations of the historical purposes of a personal God. In repentance and supplication as in joy and adoration, the songs of ancient Israel read christologically were the chosen language of prayer of the Reformed Church.

97

In contrast to both scholastics and Anabaptists, Calvin argued for the substantial identity of God's revelation to the ancient Hebrews and that to the Christians. All true revelation of whatever age is of the Christ, the eternal Son, including Old Testament visions, angelic messengers, prophetic declarations. The faithful sons of the Old Covenant actually received the benefits of the Messiah's cross and resurrection. Israel was the real church; her sacrifices were real sacraments of the Christ, his life and power. The new covenant in Christ Jesus, to be sure, is clearer, more vivid, less encumbered with ceremonies and cult, but Christ is the substance of both covenants. The Old Testament and thus the Psalms were interpreted christologically and as prophetic of the life of the church. Political and cultic references in the Psalms which seem archaic and irrelevant to a modern congregation were understood by the sixteenth-century Reformed Church at once as metaphorical prophetic allusions to her own life.

The Psalms were so thoroughly known to the Huguenots that for every occasion an apposite verse seemed to leap to the tongue. All over France, where Huguenots were confined, sometimes by the score, guards and jailers became familiar with the Psalms. The colporteurs who carried the psalters, with Bibles and catechisms, all over France, were frequently caught and burned. Many martyrs died with the words of the Apostles' Creed, but it is surprising to see what a range of the psalter was drawn on by others.

The courage and joy of these martyrs, who like the ancient Christians could have had release for a word, won converts among the onlookers. The authorities tried gags, but the cord would burn and from out of the smoke the Psalm would again begin. The bishops then ordered that the tongues of the Huguenots be cut out before they were burned. This became the general practice. At Orange pieces were torn from the Bible and psalters and forced into the mouths and wounds of the victims. "Eat your fill; tell your God to come rescue you."

When the fifty-seven Protestants of Meaux were led off to the dungeon, they lamented:

> O God, the heathen have come into thy inheritance;
>   they have defiled thy holy temple;
>   they have laid Jerusalem in ruins.
> They have given the bodies of thy servants
>   to the birds of the air for food,
>   the flesh of thy saints to the beasts of the earth (Ps. 79:1-2).

The fourteen of them who were later led out to execution sang on from the same Psalm until their tongues were cut out:

> Why should the nations say,
>   "Where is their God?"
> Let the avenging of the outpoured blood of thy servants
>   be known among the nations before our eyes!
> Let the groans of the prisoners come before thee;
>   according to thy great power preserve those doomed to die!
>   (vv. 9-10).

When armed resistance began, Psalm 68 became the "Huguenot Marseillaise":

> Let God arise, let his enemies be scattered;
>   let those who hate him flee before him!
> As smoke is driven away, so drive them away;
>   as wax melts before fire,
>   let the wicked perish before God!

At the battle of Coutras, the Reformed soldiers knelt and prayed and sang. Observing this, Roman Catholic courtiers cried out that they were afraid and were confessing, but a more experienced officer said it was not so. They were singing:

> This is the day which the Lord has made;
>   let us rejoice and be glad in it.
> Save us, we beseech Thee, O Lord!
>   O Lord, we beseech Thee, give us success! (Ps. 118:24-25).

To know and love the Psalms was the mark of a Protestant. The use of the psalter became a significant issue in the long nibbling away of the assurances of the Edict of Nantes. In 1623 singing of Psalms was forbidden in streets and shops. In 1657 it was prohibited at executions; in 1658 anywhere outside "temples," as Protestant places of worship were called. In 1659 Psalms could not even be sung privately if audible outside, and in 1661 the singing of Psalms anywhere in French territory became a felony.

There were other sung prayers than the Psalms in the Calvinist service. The Song of Simeon was used as the hymn of thanksgiving after the body and blood of Christ was received at the communion. The Ten Commandments were also set to music in French quatrains, with a *Kyrie eleison* (retained in Greek) as a prayer after each quatrain. The Lord's summary of the law is given a musical setting in some editions of the Huguenot psalter, as is the Lord's Prayer. And finally, one congregational act which was not biblical in form, but wholly so in substance, was the singing of the Apostles' Creed. In the Middle Ages, the Apostles' Creed had generally been used only in baptism, and then in Latin. The Reformation saw a great expansion in its use, Calvin desiring it in every Lord's day service in the vernacular as a congregational act. It was still continued in the baptismal service, of course, and used also in the weekday services and in family devotions and as a staple of religious education.

Such was the congregational song liturgy in Calvin's service. The other prayers were spoken by the minister. Most of them were set prayers, although there was more freedom for variation than in any other major liturgical tradition of the time. But Calvin did not consider it wise to leave all to the discretion of each individual minister.

Standing at the table (in Strassburg), the minister opened the service with the solemn adjuration from the mass: "Our help is in the Name of the Lord, who made heaven and earth. Amen." There followed at once the prayer of confession as a congregational act. This replaced the private confession of the priest before the mass, for here was a congregational priesthood. The form of a general confession was probably derived from the medieval communion orders and, like those, presupposed personal and specific confession outside the service. The general confession was to gather up and summarize the perpetual repentance of the whole people. They knelt at the pastor's call (with all Calvin's recognition of the necessary freedom and variety in such matters it was hard for him to conceive of any other posture in prayer). The words that Calvin adopted from Butzer were used thereafter by the Huguenot church and with slight variations by the Scots:

> Lord God, Almighty and everlasting Father, we acknowledge and confess, before thy Holy Majesty, that we are poor sinners, born in corruption, inclined to evil, unable by ourselves to do good, and that every day and in many ways we transgress thy holy commandments, thus calling upon ourselves by thy just judgment, condemnation and death.
>
> But, O Lord, we are grieved because we have offended thee; we condemn ourselves and our sins in solemn repentance, we turn again to thy grace and implore thee to succor us in our distress. Have pity upon us, Gracious God, Father of mercies, and pardon our sins, for the love of Jesus Christ, thy Son, our Savior.
>
> Grant to us and increase in us continually the graces of thy Holy Spirit, so that, acknowledging our faults more and more, we may grieve over them and renounce them with all our heart, and may bear the fruits of righteousness and of holiness, which may be well pleasing in thy sight, through Jesus Christ our Lord. Amen.

Then to the kneeling congregation the minister read some scriptural promises of forgiveness. Butzer used I Timothy 1:15, John 3:16, 35f., Acts 10:43, or I John 2:1,2. Then came, in the Strassburg form of Calvin's service, the absolution:

> Let each one of you acknowledge himself truly a sinner,

humbling himself before God, and believe that the heavenly
Father desires to be gracious to him in Jesus Christ;

To all who in this manner repent and seek Jesus Christ for
their salvation, I declare absolution in the name of the Father,
the Son, and the Holy Spirit. Amen.

When Calvin went back to Geneva he found there some
resistance to an absolution on the part of those who
associated it with Roman abuses. "I yielded too easily," he
later confessed; and the Geneva congregation, by beginning
to rise before the end of the confession, gave him no
chance to repair the omission. But he left on record his
judgment that an absolution should be included as at
Strassburg.

Then the congregation rose to sing the Ten Commandments and the *Kyries*. In most Lutheran liturgies—and in
the Reformed services based on the preaching orders—the
commandments were used *before* the confession as guide
for self-examination and accusation of conscience. Calvin
rather used them *after* the absolution as guide for the
grateful obedience of the forgiven Christian, a use that
many Lutherans considered dangerously near to works
righteousness. The Ten Commandments and *Kyries* were
dropped, or at least made an alternative to a Psalm, when
Calvin returned to Geneva, but most Reformed liturgies
used them, and they were restored in the French liturgy in
1639.

During the singing the minister left the table for the
pulpit. There he prepared for the reading and preaching of
the word by a prayer for the illumination of the Holy
Spirit, that the word might indeed cleave to the quick.
This is one of the two prayers of the service that was free,
and even for this some typical prayers were provided. The
other prayer at the minister's discretion was the prayer
after the sermon, which in Calvin's custom was a bidding
prayer, resuming the themes of the preached word in the
form of petitions.

After the sermon and sermon prayer the minister returned to the table, in the Strassburg usage, and the people knelt for the great prayer of intercession, for those bearing political responsibility, for pastors and the church at large, for all men and especially for those suffering affliction under war, epidemic, famine, poverty. This prayer at first concluded with a paraphrase of the Lord's Prayer, a medieval practice that both Calvin and Luther adopted. From 1545 the Lord's Prayer itself was used instead, and in some Reformed churches it was sung by the congregation.

Then the congregation rose to sing the Apostles' Creed, while the minister prepared the bread and cup at the table for the third essential element of every assembly of the church. Or rather, such was Calvin's unfulfilled desire. From the beginning to the end of his ministry, at Strassburg and at Geneva, Calvin appealed to patristic practice and sought to join the word preached and Holy Communion at every Lord's day service. But in Strassburg he was able to effect this only monthly, and in Geneva it was at first observed only three times a year, then quarterly. Calvin reluctantly accepted what he considered a seriously defective custom, but he took care to put his protest on record in the hope of future amendment. His order was always a truncated eucharistic service, at the least.

*　　　*　　　*

Calvin's concern for weekly communion contrasted with Zwingli's contentment with the preached word at all but quarterly festivals. This difference was related also to their divergent understandings of the meaning of the sacrament. For Zwingli the Lord's supper was primarily a dramatic reenactment of Jesus Christ's atoning death enjoined upon his followers as a means of quickening their faith. For Calvin, too, the memorial element was important and was ritually stressed beyond other forms by the minister reenacting Jesus' own symbolism of the last supper in the full sight of the congregation. Alone of the major Protestant traditions, the Reformed recovered the power of the biblical and patristic ceremonial. But Calvin could be shocked by Zwingli's language about the sacrament and was in essentials closer to Luther. For Calvin the most important meaning of the sacrament was the mystical union of the faithful with the actually present risen Lord in his glorified humanity. He rejected all the theories of transubstantiated or transfused "substances," but he was emphatic on the real presence to his church of the Lord of life. This enjoyment of communion with God was something prior to and distinct from the appropriation of his gifts of forgiveness and new life.

With this understanding of the Lord's supper Calvin had to insist on some form of closed communion. This was, in fact, the nerve of his concern for discipline in the church, that holy things be approached only in due reverence. Not that men could ever make themselves worthy to come into the presence of God. Quite the contrary, "we do not come to declare that we are perfect or righteous in ourselves, but ... by seeking our life in Christ, we confess that we are in death. ... All the worthiness which our Savior requires in us is to know ourselves, so as to be dissatisfied with our vices, and have all our pleasure, joy and contentment in him alone."

This requires that men be prepared for such a meeting. At Strassburg Calvin required all who expected to take communion to confer with the pastor beforehand. He wished to be sure that they understood the meaning of the sacrament, to warn those living in open sin or hatred, to comfort those in anxiety with the assurance of God's promises. This was his equivalent to the papal discipline of confession and penance, and he would have desired to keep it. The general confession and absolution at the beginning of the service was to catch up and comprehend all these preparatory spiritual conferences with individuals in terms of their particular sins and weakness of faith, which might well have been dealt with in conferences with the pastor.

The so-called "fencing" of the table, which was to become particularly associated with the Reformed tradition, was a common element in medieval communion orders and not a Reformed invention. In Calvin's service it was located after the reading of the scriptural warrant and promise from I Corinthians, when the pastor warned all those of scandalous life or without faith or understanding of the gospel not to come to the table. The service had been announced the previous week, so that "each might prepare himself to receive it worthily and with becoming reverence." The listing of sins and crimes generally strikes the modern ear as unedifying, and these portions of the liturgy, as in the Book of Common Prayer, are often omitted. But "fencing" was general pre-Reformation practice and reflects the situation of a state church wherein it was difficult to find a way for the exercise of discipline by the church apart from the magistrate, and where the total population were expected in church.

The preliminary exhortation to Calvin's liturgy ended with an expansion of the ancient response:

> Lift up your hearts.
> We lift them up unto the Lord.

This motif evidently derived from Farel rather than Butzer, and became a characteristic note in the Reformed liturgies. The doctrine of the ascension was stressed in the Reformed tradition, and the liturgies were fuller and more explicit on this theme than those who simply repeated the responsive form of the *sursum corda*. There was usually a polemic reference by way of criticism of devotion focussed on the material objects, and a summons to the congregation to address themselves to the reigning Lord of life.

> Let us raise our hearts and minds on high, where Jesus Christ is, in the glory of his Father, and from whence we look for

him at our redemption. . . . Then only will our souls be disposed to be nourished and vivified with his substance, when they are thus raised above all terrestrial objects, and carried as high as heaven, to enter the Kingdom of God, where He dwells.

"This Kingdom," Calvin had explained (*Inst.* IV,xvii, 18), "is neither bounded by location in space nor circumscribed by any limits. Thus Christ is not prevented from exerting his power wherever he pleases, in heaven and on earth. He shows his presence in power and strength, is always among his own people, and breathes his life upon them, and lives in them, sustaining them, strengthening, quickening, keeping them unharmed, as if he were present in the body. In short, he feeds his people with his own body, the communion of which he bestows upon them by the power of his Spirit."

At the actual distribution the Reformed churches followed at least three distinct types of ceremonial. Calvin, the French and German Reformed, had the people come forward in line to receive standing at the table, usually the bread at one corner and the wine at the other. The Scots and Dutch preferred à Lasco's ceremony of serving the people seated at long tables on the nave. And the Zwinglians and Anglicans served the people in their places. Calvin refused to make an issue of whether the bread and cup were to go from hand to hand, or to be served to each individual by a minister, or whether the wine be white or red (it never occurred to him that it might be unfermented) or the bread leavened or unleavened. Such matters were indifferent and left to the discretion of the church (*Inst.* IV,xvii,43).

The words of distribution were:

Take, eat, the body of Jesus which has been delivered unto death for you.

This is the cup of the new testament in the blood of Jesus which has been shed for you.

Those who read later pietism back into the sixteenth century and suppose the Reformers to have been preoccupied with an introverted and individualistic penitence should observe the substitution made at Strassburg for the "Lamb of God" of the mass. During the actual distribution of the elements the Strassburg congregation sang one of the triumph songs from the psalter, Psalm 138, read christologically. A petition for individual forgiveness was replaced by the church's triumph in the accomplished victory of the Son. Each of the three stanzas of the French metrical version ends with "Hallelujah! Hallelujah!" Then the minister gave thanks in language, which, originally from Butzer's second prayer, was to come down in both the Huguenot and Scottish services of communion:

> Heavenly Father, we give thee undying praise and thanks for the great blessing which thou hast conferred upon us miserable sinners, in bringing us to partake of thy Son Jesus Christ,
>> whom thou didst suffer to be delivered to death for us,
>> and now impartest to us as the food of everlasting life.
> Now, in continuance of thy goodness towards us, never allow us to become forgetful of these things, but grant rather, that
>> carrying them about engraven on our hearts,
> we may profit and increase in a faith effectual to every good work. Hence, too, may we dedicate the remainder of our life to the advancement of thy glory and the edification of our neighbors,
>> thru the same Jesus Christ thy Son, who in the unity of the Holy Spirit, liveth with thee and reigneth forever. Amen.

The congregation rose from their knees to sing Simeon's song,

> Lord, now lettest thou thy servant depart in peace
> For mine eyes have seen thy salvation

and received the blessing from the Book of Numbers,

> The Lord bless you and keep you
> The Lord make his face shine upon you
>> and be gracious unto you. . . .

107

and was finally dismissed with a word about alms:

Remember Jesus Christ in his little ones.

This fourth and last necessary element in the service, the giving of alms, was thus appointed for the conclusion as the people left the service. There was no ceremonial presentation at an "altar"; the Reformers feared the religious consequences that had been drawn from the offering and oblation of the mass.

*   *   *

Three of four observations by way of conclusion. One must be on guard, first of all, against according more authority to Calvin's service than he himself intended. Calvin did not believe in permitting great freedom to the individual minister or congregation on these matters, but he left great freedom to the church authorities of a given region. He actually suggested that liturgical variety was desirable in order to show that the unity of the church does not consist in such things.

Formally, the Calvinist order is marked by its insistence on the unity and balance of word and sacrament. Calvin's followers would be unable to maintain this balance. There have been Christian groups which have virtually lost the preaching of the word, and others who have lost nearly everything else. Calvin was wiser.

It must also be remembered that the Calvinist service was the liturgy of a disciplined congregation and has necessary presuppositions of instruction, commitment, and weekday Christian obedience. The distinctive quality of Calvinist worship was more influenced by the character of the congregation than by the literary or musical vehicles of its praise. To abstract the prayers from this very specific social context and to study them in terms of literary quality or historical provenance misses precisely their liturgical meaning. The bias of many historians is peculiarly unfortunate in the case of a tradition such as the Reformed. And to emulate the Calvinist model truly, one must consider the teaching, discipline, witness, and work of the congregation in relation to the worship.

VII

THE LITURGICAL ORIGINS
OF THE REFORMED CHURCHES

HOWARD HAGEMAN

In beginning a consideration of the liturgical origins of the Reformed churches of the Dutch churches, we do well to remind ourselves that the Dutch church was in every way a "johnny-come-lately" upon the Reformation scene. It did not spring straight from the forehead of John Calvin. In fact, the great Reformer, himself of the second genera-

~~~~~~

Howard Hageman is pastor of the North Church (Reformed Church of America), Newark, New Jersey. He received the D.D. degree from Central College in 1957, and has lectured at New Brunswick, Bloomfield, and Princeton Theological Seminaries, as well as in South Africa. He has served as President of the General Synod of the Reformed Church of America, and edits a column in the denominational weekly, **Church Herald.** *He is also a contributing editor of* **The Reformed Journal.** *Among his books are* **Lily Among the Thorns, Pulpit and Table, Predestination, That the World May Know,** *and* **Advice to Mature Christians.**

tion, had been in his grave several years when the first embryonic structure of the Dutch Reformed Church appeared in 1568. In other words, by the time the Dutch church had begun to work out its patterns, a number of possibilities, directions and influences were open to it.

To begin at what might seem to be the beginning, the ancestor of its liturgy was a volume published by Petrus Dathenus in 1566 in the German city of Frankenthal. In this volume were a metrical version of the Psalms, mostly the work of Dathenus himself, a Dutch translation of the Heidelberg Catechism, then only three years old, and finally a section entitled "forms and prayers as they are used by us." These "forms and prayers" are the first Dutch version of what are the oldest parts of the liturgy of the Dutch Reformed churches.

But to get back to Frankenthal in 1566 is to reach only the initial point in the search. Who was Petrus Dathenus? Why was there a Dutch congregation in the German city of Frankenthal? And when Dathenus published his volume in 1566, from where did he get his forms and prayers? Were they his own composition or was he drawing on other sources?

At first the answer to our last question may seem very close at hand. Frankenthal was a city in the Rhine-Palatinate, the dominion of the pious Elector Frederick, who, in order to end the strife between Lutheran and Reformed in his territory, had ordered two of his court chaplains to draft a new catechism. This appeared in 1563, and it is known as the Heidelberg Catechism. That accounts for its appearance in Dathenus' little volume of 1566. As a refugee minister in Frederick's territory, Dathenus would doubtless have felt obliged to give the elector's catechism every chance, quite apart from its own intrinsic merits.

But it also accounts, at least immediately, for Dathenus' forms and prayers. For it is not commonly remembered that Frederick's forms for unity included not only a catechism but a liturgy and a church order as well. While there

111

are some omissions and a few alterations, even a hasty look will reveal that Dathenus' forms and prayers are, for the most part, nothing but a Dutch translation of a German original, the so-called Palatinate liturgy, the twin to the Heidelberg Catechism. While he was translating the cate-chism for the use of his Dutch congregation in Franken-thal, Dathenus obviously continued and translated the liturgy, or large parts of it, as well. So it is not only the catechetical origins of the Dutch Reformed churches, but also their liturgical origins that were in Heidelberg.

But now we have really pushed our original inquiry only one step further back. If Dathenus took his liturgical materials from Heidelberg, where did Heidelberg get them? Were they original or were they reworkings of previous materials? To answer that question we shall have to take a trip through a good deal of sixteenth-century Europe be-fore returning to Frankenthal.

The first Dutch Protestant congregation in the world was organized in the city of London in 1550. I use the word "Protestant" intentionally, because the Reformed character of this congregation was not entirely clear at the outset. While the southern Netherlands (including a good deal of present-day Belgium) was by this time largely—to the extent that it was Protestant—Calvinist, the northern Netherlands was still largely Mennonite and Lutheran. In any event, about four thousand of these people fled from the Spanish terror to England where in 1550 King Edward VI gave them an unused Augustinian monastery in London and allowed them to organize a church.

Though one church, the London group worshipped as two congregations, one French-speaking, the other Dutch. The French congregation was led by Vallerand Pullain, Calvin's successor as minister of the congregation of French refugees in Strassburg. In fact, he had come to London with a good bit of his congregation in 1549 because of Lutheran pressures in Strassburg. Because the English authorities required complete information about the life and order of these refugee congregations, Pullain presented to them his *Liturgia Sacra*, which was the same liturgy Calvin had drafted for the use of the congregation in Strassburg when he was there.

For the Dutch group, however, the story is a little more complicated and to me, at least, somewhat confused. The leader of the Dutch section was that fascinating Polish nobleman, John à Lasco. I should like to insert a few words about à Lasco not only because his greatness is usually neglected in history but also because of how he illustrates the truly nationless quality of the Reformation. A Polish nobleman by birth, he was partly educated in France where he became acquainted with the work of Zwingli and so learned evangelical theology from the Zwinglian point of view. Returning to Poland, he became dean of Gnesen and ultimately bishop of Vesprin (at least he was elected to the latter office; whether or not he served in it is not quite clear). Forced to leave Poland because of his evangelical views (up to this point, mind you, an announced Zwinglian had been dean and possibly bishop in the Roman Catholic Church!) he crossed the border into Germany in 1540 to serve the congregation in Emden. After a short term there he became superintendent of the church in East Friesland and in 1543 accepted the invitation of the Countess Anna to organize the Reformed Church in Oldenburg. From there he came to London in 1549 at the joint invitation of Archbishop Cranmer and King Edward to take charge of the rapidly growing congregation of Dutch refugees.

Once again the English authorities required, among other things, the submission of a liturgy. But here the problem was different from that of the French section. The French had a liturgical tradition of almost ten years. Pullain had only to bring it with him, revise it slightly to fit the English situation, and present it. The Dutch had none. It was one of à Lasco's first tasks to create one.

The most obvious thing to do would have been to

113

translate the French liturgy into Dutch. *That* he did not do and we can only speculate as to the reasons why. For one thing, I imagine the Dutch section of the church contained a good many Mennonites or sympathizers with that point of view. For them any liturgy was suspect, but that of Calvin was probably too catholic even to be considered. But we also have to consider the probable attitude of à Lasco himself. He was, after all, a confirmed Zwinglian and, though he never expressed himself on it, he would doubtless have felt that Pullain's liturgy, with its emphasis on the frequent celebration of the Lord's supper and its strong theology of the real presence, was something with which he could not be happy. In any event, for the Dutch part of the London congregation, without liturgical tradition as it was, he set to work to compose his own liturgy.

The puzzle is to know exactly what it was that the Dutch part of the congregation used. The congregation was scattered after Edward's death in 1553. Pullain's *Liturgia Sacra* had been published in London in 1551. But à Lasco's work was not published until 1555, and then in Frankfurt. It is an imposing volume entitled *Forma ac Ratio tota Ecclesiastici ministerii in peregrinorum potissimum vero Germanorum Ecclesia instituta Londini in Anglia.* The liturgical section is of extreme length, long enough to make one wonder whether even in those days it could actually have been used in a congregation. But it could well be that in preparing the work for publication in Frankfurt à Lasco embellished and extended what had in actual usage in London been simpler or shorter.

We could assume with Mensinga, the classic historian of Dutch Reformed liturgy, that during the London years à Lasco used only a handwritten copy of his forms (there was no active congregational participation), which he later, in exile, elaborated for publication, were it not for the existence of another volume published somewhere in Germany in 1554, a year earlier than à Lasco's volume appeared. The author, Martinus Micronius (Maarten Klein), had been an elder in the London congregation. The full title page reads (in translation):

> Christian Ordinances of the Netherlands congregation of Christ which was established in London in 1550 by the Christian prince, King Edward VI; faithfully collected and published by M. Micron with the consent of the elders and deacons of the congregation of Christ in London; for the comfort and profit of all believers.

Micron's work, like à Lasco's, is an entire church order. The liturgical portions are obviously a shortened version in Dutch of à Lasco's longer Latin work. We shall return to it later, but the riddle that has never really been answered is what liturgy the Dutch congregation in London used during the few years of its existence. Did it use a Dutch translation of à Lasco's *Forma ac Ratio,* which some historians assert was published in London, though no copy of it has ever been found? Or did it use Micron's abridged form? Or was there only a handwritten Dutch copy of à Lasco's work that both à Lasco and Micron tried to reconstruct after the London congregation had broken up?

Whatever the case may be, for the rest of our story à Lasco's *Forma ac Ratio* remains a museum piece, though a very interesting one indeed. Micron's "Christian Ordinances" is the liturgical tradition that went with the Dutch congregation into exile. Perhaps we should have a brief look at its liturgical portion before we leave London. The Calvinist (and catholic) character of Pullain's *Liturgia Sacra* may be clearly seen from the first two items in his book—the order of service for Sunday morning and the order for the Lord's supper. Mensinga's comment on this is somewhat naive:

> The placing of the Communion Liturgy immediately after the liturgy for Sunday morning and not next to baptism is remarkable. It is still the idea of the mass, namely that the Supper ought to be celebrated every Sunday.

It is hard to believe that our nineteenth-century scholar

was not aware that it was also the idea of John Calvin, and that in laying out his liturgy Pullain was doing nothing more than reasserting the tradition he learned from his master at Strassburg!

Micron's *Christian Ordinances* (reflecting à Lasco's concepts) show a very different arrangement. The table of contents shows a certain logic, but it is hardly Calvin's. The first items relate to ordinations, and then it continues as follows:

9. The order and way of preaching and common prayer
10. Instruction of children
11. The admission of children to the Supper
12. Prophesying and testing doctrine
13. Baptism
14. The Supper

(If Micron's logic was what I think it was, I wonder why baptism is placed after the instruction of children. But that takes us off in another direction.) The point to notice is the very Zwinglian way in which preaching and the Lord's supper are separated. Of course, there is nothing strange about this: à Lasco was Zwinglian, and his liturgy could have been expected to reflect these views. What is amazing, however, is to contemplate that refugee congregation in London, French and Dutch, using two completely different liturgical traditions under one roof.

What is more, the congregation took these two traditions with it when it was scattered by the accession of Mary Tudor to the English throne. Its peregrinations are a little difficult to trace but they seem to have gone about as follows. After a brief and unhappy stay in Denmark and various cities in northern Germany, the refugees were finally welcomed in the German city of Emden. Accommodations proved too small for the entire group, however, so a part moved on to Frankfurt. After seven years there, however, the Lutherans made their lives so miserable (they were not allowed to worship inside the city walls, to vote, to hold office, etc.) that some took quick advantage of

Elector Frederick's offer to settle in his domain, and so came to Frankenthal. (So far as I have been able to determine, incidentally, the French group remained in Frankfurt despite the inconveniences. There is still a French Reformed congregation there to this day.)

The Frankenthal group was small: two shiploads of about sixty Dutch families, who arrived there in 1562. The leader under whose guidance they left Frankfurt and accepted the elector's invitation to settle in Frankenthal was Petrus Dathenus.

We have taken this liturgical tour simply to point out that by the time Ursinus and Olevianus came to prepare their liturgy for the Elector Frederick in 1563, the two liturgical traditions of the Netherlands refugees were well known in Germany, if not in the Palatinate. Pullain's *Liturgia Sacra*, representing the Calvinist tradition, was available in Frankfurt, where it was published both in 1554 and 1555; and both à Lasco's *Forma ac Ratio* and Micron's *Christian Ordinances*, representing the Zwinglian tradition, were also available in German editions. The evidence seems to be that these actually were the sources used by the Heidelberg compilers. Calvin's Genevan service received its first German edition in 1563, the very year the Heidelberg liturgy was published. It would be much more reasonable to suppose that it was Pullain's version that was used for the Calvinistic strain. There is no evidence to suggest that they knew Zwingli's *Church Order*, but the Palatinate liturgy borrows from Micron's *Christian Ordinances* numerous times. (The only other Reformed source used is an occasional line from one of Oecolampadius' early liturgies in Basel, which either Ursinus or Olevianus could have had on his library shelf from student days.)

We are then faced with the strong possibility that the Palatinate liturgy, the original of the Dutch liturgy of 1566, was a deliberate attempt to fuse both Calvinistic and Zwinglian traditions into a single unity. The possibility becomes all the stronger when we remember the irenic

117

spirit that lay behind the whole endeavor of catechism, church order, and liturgy—the desire to provide forms of unity for a badly divided people.

But when one sits down with the forms and begins to trace out their borrowings from Pullain and Micron, one soon becomes aware of a large block of material that can be traced to neither. The first impulse would be to assign it to the originality of one or both of the authors. But before we do that, we must remember that there were also Lutherans in Frederick's realm. Would it have been possible to include them also by employing something from one of their liturgical traditions?

Knowing the strong liturgical conservatism of Lutheranism even then, that hardly seems possible. But by what can only be called a freak, it was. In the principality of Württemberg, the church was something of a maverick (and I understand still is). Strongly Lutheran in its doctrine, it was almost as strongly Reformed in its liturgy. Perhaps that is an unfair characterization, but the fact remains that the liturgy of Württemberg has nothing to do with the Lutheran reshaping of the mass, but makes provision for a simple preaching service with an appended Supper, largely didactic in tone. The earliest edition of which we have any record was published in Tübingen in 1561 and must therefore have been available to Ursinus and Olevianus in Heidelberg in 1563. At any rate, in many places they made very generous use of it!

In a moment we shall take a look at the wondrous composition of Lutheran, Calvinist, and Zwinglian strands that constitutes the liturgical ancestry of the Dutch Reformed churches. But before we leave its history, consider the strange way in which liturgies prepared for the refugee congregation in London became the source for a liturgy in Heidelberg which in turn became the original for the liturgy for the same Netherlands church that had tried fifteen years earlier to establish itself on British soil. A fascinating liturgical round trip.

118

Before we proceed further with our investigations, however, let us take a look at what would have taken place in one of Dathenus' congregations. To give the full picture, we shall assume it is one of the occasions on which the Lord's supper was celebrated. Dathenus gives us very little assistance here. For the worship of the congregation on the Lord's day his book contains only three items, two fairly long prayers, one to be used before the sermon, the other after it, and the form for dismissing the congregation, in this case the so-called Aaronic benediction. It should also be noted that the second prayer, the prayer after the sermon, terminates in the Lord's Prayer.

The order for the Lord's supper is exactly that used in the so-called unabridged form in the liturgy of the Dutch Reformed churches today. It begins with the recitation of Paul's version of the words of institution, followed by a long didactic passage, then a short prayer and the Lord's Prayer, after which the Apostles' Creed is introduced with a form of prayer. Then comes a paraphrase of the *sursum corda*, the words of distribution, and the actual communion. The thanksgiving after communion is Psalm 103, followed by a short prayer of thanksgiving and the Lord's Prayer. Presumably a closing Psalm was sung before the benediction was pronounced.

We can get a better idea of the Sunday service in these days, however, by following through the ways in which various synods dealt with Dathenus' forms down to the great Synod of Dort, which pretty well fixed things for the next few centuries. It was 1568 before the first synod of refugee congregations could be held. Dathenus was its moderator. (It will be remembered that his liturgical work had been in print as early as 1566.) No synodical action seems to have been taken. It is probable that the prestige of the editor, together with the already widespread use of the book, had already assured its position. It was the Synod of 1574, meeting in Dort, which made two alterations that interest us. For one thing, this Synod directed

119

that even as worship on the Lord's day had a fixed ending, so it should have a fixed beginning, the words of Psalm 124:8, "Our help is in the Name of the Lord who made heaven and earth." These had been the opening words in Calvin's liturgy as indeed in the Roman mass. (Oddly, all later editions of the liturgy omit this votum, as it came to be called. I rather suspect that this omission was not intended to say anything more than that use of the votum was so universal as to require no mention.)

The other alteration involved Dathenus' prayer after the sermon. Even in that day the Synod deemed that the prayer was too long, better suited for days of fasting and penitence. It substituted a prayer from the liturgy of Geneva, thus providing not only a shorter prayer but one of a better character, as we shall see when we come to analyze these forms. (Dathenus must have approved. He was again moderator of the Synod which met at Dort in 1578 and the alteration of his prayer was not discussed.)

A liturgical question that repeatedly engaged the attention of all these earlier synods was the relation of the reading of Scripture to preaching. Evidently there were many, and with understandable reasons, who persisted in the use of the ancient Roman lectionaries with an Epistle and Gospel. Lekkerkerker has collected a number of synodical utterances on this question:

> *Dort, 1574*: Regarding the Sunday gospels which are in use in the Church of Rome, it was decided that they shall not be preached in our churches, but an entire book of Holy Scripture shall be usefully explained in an orderly way. . . .

> *Dort, 1578:* And in places where the Sunday gospels are still in use, they shall be tolerated until such time as they can be skilfully set aside.

> *Middelburg, 1581:* Is it right to use the Sunday gospels to enlighten the people? *Answer:* it is better that an entire book of the Old or New Testaments, not a piece here or there, be used, provided that the book chosen is suited to the need of the church.

These synodical actions reveal two things. One is the persistent way in which the use of the traditional pericopes hung on, despite repeated actions by successive synods. I understand that in Friesland they continued in use right into the nineteenth century. But the more important observation is the way in which these early Dutch synods reaffirmed the Reformed concept of reading and preaching of the word as a single act, best carried out by the use of *lectio continua*, the continuous exposition of a book of Scripture.

It is interesting to observe that these early liturgies omit three items generally thought of as key portions of the Dutch Reformed tradition in worship: the creed, the law, and the salutation. The fate of the creed is quite easy to trace. The earlier editions of the liturgy all place it at the conclusion to the prayer before the sermon, introduced by words such as these:

> Strengthen us also in the true Christian faith, that we may more and more cling to it, whereof we now make confession with mouth and heart, saying, I believe, etc.

The Synod of Dort removed it from this place in 1619, relocating it in the afternoon service, which was a teaching service. The synod felt (I think wrongly) that the creed was a teaching instrument more than an act of affirmation; hence the new placing.

The law is somewhat more difficult to trace. Not only did it occupy a prominent place in Calvin's liturgy; it can be found in both Zwingli's and à Lasco's as well. Indeed, it had a wide use in pre-Reformation Europe, especially in its Germanic portions, because of the popularity of the *Prone*, a little devotional service in the vernacular that often served as a preface to the mass. In this service the decalogue also played a prominent part. What happened to it in Dathenus' service book?

We know that it was used in worship, because the Synod of Dort of 1619, which decided that the creed should be used in the afternoon, decided that the law should be used in the morning. There is also evidence of its use in an edition of the Bible, liturgy, and Psalms printed in Leiden in 1596. The editor inserted a short commentary on Sunday worship stating clearly that the Ten Commandments were read or sung as part of the Sunday morning service.

This little commentary leads me to believe that the decalogue is not mentioned by Dathenus because it was not something that the minister read, but something that the congregation sang. Since Dathenus nowhere gives any directions for congregational singing, which nevertheless forms a very significant part of Reformed liturgy, I assume that so widespread a usage, especially among congregations of a Calvinistic descent, would have been one of those things which could have been taken for granted.

The salutation has to be the object of another educated guess. It has a long history in Christian liturgy, where it has always served as a call to prayer. The little antiphony "The Lord be with you"/"And with thy spirit" is, I suppose, the best-known example. Why Calvin chose to begin his liturgy with the votum I have no idea. The Palatinate liturgy that served Dathenus as a model begins with a salutation, followed directly, as it should be, by prayer.

My guess is that in the earliest day both usages were followed to begin the service. Apparently the decision of the Synod of 1574 to use the votum exclusively was an effort, never quite successful, to bring some order to the situation. The salutation has survived among American Reformed churches, although in the Netherlands (and in South Africa) the usual custom is to use the votum and the salutation back to back. Both of these traditions are thus present and accounted for.

With this look at synodical actions, records of tradition, and Dathenus' two prayers, we can begin to reconstruct a service in Amsterdam of 1600. The service would begin with the singing of a Psalm, led by a *voorlezer*, who would hold up a placard on which the number was written.

(There were organs in church buildings, but at this time they were used only for concert purposes.) During the Psalm the *domine* and the elders would enter and take their places. At its conclusion the *domine* would use the votum, or the salutation, or perhaps both, to call the people to prayer. Thereafter he would use Dathenus' prayer before the sermon, a prayer of confession and for the right hearing of the word, which would conclude with the Apostles' Creed, said by the congregation in a kind of low mumble.

At this point, I imagine, the congregation would sing the Ten Commandments, after which the *domine* would give himself to the reading and preaching of the word. I say "I imagine" because there are one or two things that give me cause to wonder about this. And so we must digress again.

One of the universal marks of Reformed liturgy in the sixteenth century was the use of an act of confession followed by words of absolution and, in many cases, of retention, the liturgical expression of the well-known power of the keys. Usually it came at the beginning of the service but sometimes, as in the case of both à Lasco and the Palatine, it came after the sermon at the end of the service. Dathenus' first prayer takes obvious account of this usage because it is largely a prayer of confession (in fact, many of the phrases in it that ask for forgiveness are stronger than a good many of the so-called "Words of Assurance" one hears nowadays). But of an absolution or retention in Dathenus there is absolutely no trace.

Apparently the question was taken up in the early days, since it was on the docket of the Synod that met at Middelburg in 1581. The decision of the Synod was that the binding and loosing of sins was sufficiently covered in the preaching of the gospel, and that there was therefore no need for any liturgical form for it. I do not know what lay behind this decision of why the question came up, but I am constrained to believe it was raised by those of Calvinist or French tradition (recall to what extent the early Reformed Church in the Netherlands was French), who missed this element in Dathenus' liturgy.

Evidently the decision of the Synod made no difference (then as now) to those who were going to do what they were going to do. In any event, the commentator in the Bible of 1596 states that, in connection with the decalogue, the *domine*, using words of Scripture, assured those who repented of their forgiveness and warned those who refused that the wrath of God still rested upon them. So, as late as 1596 the use of an absolution and retention must have been common enough to have warranted this kind of comment. I suspect that it was never set down because it would have horrified the large contingent of ex-Mennonites still included in the Reformed Church at that time, just as its use today horrifies the large number of Baptists in the Reformed Church today.

To return to the service of 1600, then, the *domine* may or may not have used such words in connection with the confession and the decalogue. In any event, he did read the Scriptures and preach. (Probably we would be hearing his twenty-third sermon on the First Book of Samuel; but if he was a stubborn Frisian, he might be preaching on the gospel for the day!) After the sermon he would use Dathenus' second prayer, perhaps preceded by the singing of a Psalm. That prayer, as altered by the Synod of 1574, was one of thanksgiving and intercession, an improvement, as I have said, over Dathenus' original, which contained no thanksgiving but another long confession of sin before the intercessions. Again the Lord's Prayer would have been said, much as the creed had been said earlier.

The Lord's supper that followed would have been exactly as the unabridged liturgy of the Reformed Churches today presents it, with one possible exception. Micron's London book and the Palatinate liturgy give the words of distribution as follows:

> The bread which we break is the communion of the body of
> Christ. Take, eat, remember, and believe that the body of our

Lord Jesus Christ was given over to the death of the cross for the forgiveness of all our sins.

The cup of blessing which we bless is the communion of the blood of Christ. Take, drink all of it, remember, and believe that the blood of our Lord Jesus Christ was poured out in death on the cross for the forgiveness of all our sins.

The earliest editions of the liturgy used today contained these words, the so-called *London aanhangsel*. In fact the Synod of 1571 allowed the minister to use either Paul's words or the words of Christ, "Take, eat, this is my body," as he saw fit. The Synod of 1574, however, took away this privilege and made Paul's words with the *London aanhangsel* obligatory. The strange thing is that there was never a synodical action changing this decision. But in both the editions of 1586 and 1619 the *London aanhangsel* is omitted. Its exact fate will probably never be known.

Before leaving this part of the inquiry, I should like to call attention to the extreme flexibility of Dathenus' provision for Sunday morning worship and to suggest a reason for it. So far as the requirements are concerned, a Sunday morning service could have consisted of nothing but the opening prayer, the sermon, the closing prayer with the Lord's Prayer, and the Benediction, with a Psalm or two sung at appropriate intervals. I have no doubt that many services had no more content than that; a visit to the Zwinglian parts of Reformed Switzerland today would reveal scores of Sunday services built according to precisely this plan.

On the other hand, by leaving the question of additions to this skeletal form completely open, a congregation could construct an order of service remarkably like that of Calvin at Strassburg or Pullain's *Liturgia Sacra*. I have tried to show from various synodical actions and the words of at least one commentator that many of them did, fleshing out Dathenus' rather meager provision with votum, law, absolution, etc.

The reason for such liberty, I suggest, goes back to the

dual inheritance from the congregation in London. Though that inheritance seems to have followed linguistic lines— the Dutch following à Lasco and the French Pullain—there can be no doubt that there was a good deal of mixing as the church in the Netherlands began to develop. After all, from the very beginning there was a sizable number of French-speaking churches in the Netherlands, some of which remain to this day. (It is from them, incidentally, that almost all the forms for ordination today stem.) Though these churches did not use Dathenus' forms but had their own liturgy derived from that of Pullain, their usages had great influence on some of the Dutch congregations, especially in larger cities. Dathenus' forms, therefore, made it possible for those who wished to be loyal to the fuller tradition of Calvinist liturgy to do so, while at the same time providing equally for those whose liturgical ideas went back from à Lasco to Zwingli.

I have indicated that the final revisions of Dathenus' work, together with the additions made by later synods, were the work of the great Synod of Dort in 1619. For the most part these were minor: the greatest revision was the addition of a form for the baptism of adults, which had hitherto not been included. The reason usually given for this addition is that the Synod was seeking to make provision for heathen converts in both the East Indies and the West, more commonly called New Netherland.

But the Synod of Dort made one addition perhaps unwittingly. When its finished work was published it was called "The Netherlands Liturgy." I have no idea what led the Synod to use this traditional Christian word as the title for its forms for worship. Not even Calvin had made use of it; he had entitled his liturgy "The Form of Prayers." So far as I can determine the only Reformation service to make use of the word, in its Latin form, had been Pullain's *Liturgia Sacra*. Whether the French congregations which used Pullain's work had begun to call it their *liturgie* or not I do not know. I wish I could say that the fathers at Dort had some compelling reason to grace the Dutch language with this French word, but I am grateful that it happened, whatever the reason. For however far we may have wandered in these centuries, the title of this book is an everlasting reminder that the forms of worship used in Reformed churches today claim to be one with the great traditions of Catholic Christendom. This is not a "book of forms," not a "book of worship," not a "ritual," but "The Liturgy."

*   *   *

Finally, let us analyze the sources Dathenus and his Palatinate original used in compiling their liturgy. Here I must confess that I am relying entirely upon the investigations of Dutch scholars of the history of the liturgy.

We can dispose of Dathenus' two Sunday morning prayers rather quickly. Mensinga says that the first prayer—the prayer of confession and for a right hearing of the word—is entirely of Dathenus' own composition. I am sure that this is true, though one wonders how completely anyone ever composes his own prayer and how much bits and pieces of other prayers, lodged in the mind unconsciously, find their way into what one supposes to be his own composition.

It is worth noting that it is the traditional Reformed custom, one here evidenced by Dathenus, to ask for the blessing of the Spirit on the word *before* its reading and preaching, not, as has so generally become the case today, afterward. This may seem a small point, but one that I think has fairly large theological dimensions.

Dathenus entitled the prayer after the sermon "A Prayer for the Whole Need of Christendom," a phrase that resembles rather strikingly the prayer "for the whole state of Christ's Church" in the Anglican liturgy. With some alterations he borrowed this from the Palatinate liturgy. The first part, another long confession of sin, had been lifted by the German liturgy almost entirely from a prayer used

127

in Geneva, while the second part, consisting of intercessions, was apparently the work of the Palatine authors
whom Dathenus translated and adapted.

Recall that the Synod of 1574 replaced this prayer with
a shorter one taken from Geneva. Not only did this prayer
replace the element of confession with thanksgiving, as we
have observed, but it also provided for some variation in
the intercessions according to special circumstances. There
was full recognition of the great part intercession plays in
the prayer of the church. If there is one outstanding
weakness in the worship of the Reformed Church today, it
is the way the prayer of the church has become the prayer
of the pastor and intercession has been replaced by anything from his own private meditation to a flank attack on
the morning sermon. In the name of free prayer this has
been too great a price to pay.

I deal rather hastily with these two prayers because they
have almost entirely disappeared from use today. But even
though in both language and content the originals have
long since become outdated, they still deserve study as
examples of what our fathers believed the prayers of the
church should contain.

I should like to devote the remainder of this essay to
analyzing the origins of the Reformed liturgy for the
Lord's supper, again depending on the scholarship of others to provide some information and to dispel some
mythology. It is commonly thought that no greater piece of
Calvinism exists than the traditional Reformed liturgy for
the Lord's supper. Let us see exactly how true this assertion is.

To begin with, the entire form is a translation from the
Palatinate liturgy of 1563. In translating this form, Dathenus made fewer alterations than anywhere else in his entire
liturgy, alterations so minor that they are not worth men-
tioning. However, an examination of the sources used by
the Palatine compilers begins to turn up some fascinating
results.

The form in question begins by narrating the events of the Last Supper as given by Paul in I Corinthians. In and of itself that may not seem surprising, but it does represent a radical departure from the common usage of Reformed tradition. Consider: this narrative of institution, being followed directly by the long didactic passage, was obviously meant to be read from the pulpit. In the customary Reformed pattern of the time the narrative of institution was always read at the table. Here (and I cannot believe it was by accident) it is shoved back in the service so that it must be read from the pulpit. In fact, if you examine the entire liturgy, the words of institution are never said from the table. At the time of distribution they are not used, but the Pauline words are substituted.

The long didactic passage that follows is divided into two parts. The first is a penitential section that includes a fencing of the table. Scholars who have gone over this section carefully say that it contains almost nothing original but is in the main a rather skilful blending of Calvin's liturgy and Micron's *Christian Ordinances*. Many of the phrases found in comparable sections of Calvin and Micron sound very familiar to those acquainted with the Reformed liturgy:

> And although we feel we have not perfect faith and do not serve God with such zeal as we are bound, but have daily to strive with the weakness of our faith and the evil lusts of our flesh, nevertheless because the Lord shows us this grace that we have this his holy gospel written in our hearts and that he grants us to live according to his righteousness and holy commandments, so let us be entirely certain that notwithstanding the sins and wickedness which remain in us, he receives us and counts us worthy partakers of this spiritual table (Calvin).

> Nevertheless, we do not say this, beloved brothers, to distress the contrite hearts of believers as though none were worthy to come to the Table of the Lord save those who were free from all sin and perfect in all holiness. For Christ the Lord did not institute his Supper to testify to our righteousness and

129

perfection, but rather to testify to our weakness and unrighteousness (Micron).

The second part of the form is a theological section, which seeks to explain the meaning of the Lord's supper. Here the unscrambling of the Palatinate sources is somewhat more difficult. The words of the form are so familiar that most people are dulled against the several rather awkward theological shifts within its relatively few paragraphs.

The section begins with a remembrance of Christ, culminating in the substitutionary atonement of his death on the cross. It is a beautiful piece of work, making full use of such effective contrasts as "He though innocent was condemned to death that we might be acquitted" and " 'My God, why hast thou forsaken me?' that we might be accepted of God and never be forsaken by him." Lekkerkerker considers it to be one of the finest parts of the entire liturgy. Save for an occasional phrase that can be ascribed to Calvin, no original for it can be found. It obviously was the work of one of the Palatinate authors. Mensinga believes that in view of its close theological and literary affinities with the Heidelberg Catechism, especially Questions 37 and 38, this section is the work of Ursinus himself, and I can find no reason to think otherwise.

"The new and eternal covenant of grace and reconciliation," with which this section concludes, provides a bridge to the next section: "that we might firmly believe that we belong, etc." For this section there is an original extant, the Lutheran Agenda of Württemberg, which had been widely used by the Lutheran community in the Rhine Palatinate, which, it must be remembered, Elector Frederick sought to include in his new catechism, church order, and liturgy of 1563. Actually the Württemberg Church Order was itself based on an even older Lutheran church order, that of Brandenburg in 1534. I said that Württemberg was the original for the Palatinate liturgy.

That is only a half-truth. The fact is that we are about to examine one of the most fascinating liturgical (and therefore theological) swindles on record.

I mentioned that Frederick's realm contained a large number of Lutherans, with whom the elector was anxious to reach an ecclesiastical peace. The liturgy most of them used was the Württemberg Church Order. It is a fair surmise, therefore, that the compilers of the new liturgy were under royal instructions to do what they could to include at least parts of Württemberg. In one sense this did not seem to be difficult since Württemberg, as we saw, was Reformed in its liturgical concept.

The trouble was that it was still soundly Lutheran theologically. What the Palatinate compilers did, therefore, was to preserve as much of the language of Württemberg as possible while completely altering its theological substance. The Lutheran liturgy had several times used the phrase "by a sure remembrance and pledge." But of what? For the Lutherans the bread and wine were a sure remembrance and pledge "that we abide in the Lord Jesus Christ and he in us and therefore that we have eternal life." The Palatinate authors altered this to say that the bread and wine were a sure remembrance and pledge that Jesus becomes to us the meat and drink of life eternal *on the cross*.

The full meaning of this alteration may not become apparent until we examine the next one. For Lutherans, the supper is a sure remembrance and pledge that Christ gives himself to us for food. For the new liturgy it is a sure remembrance and pledge that he feeds and satisfies our hungry and thirsty souls. The difference may not seem great until we ask *how*. The Palatinate product answers that question. Through his death on the cross he has taken away the cause of our hunger, that is, sin.

It takes little theological insight to perceive that here we are dealing with the basic idea of Zwinglianism, the notion that the only value in the supper is in making us remember

131

the atoning death of Christ on Calvary. The foundation has been laid in Ursinus' (if it is his) lovely opening section of the atonement. Now here in the supper we have the instrument by which this remembrance is made possible. What Christ gives us at the table is a closer view of his death and passion. What satisfies our hunger and thirst is the remembrance that he has died for us. The Lutheran form of words may still be here but its content has been changed to say something quite different.

Now of course the Zwinglian view of the supper is a perfectly logical one, but it does not happen to be the official view of the Reformed Church. We shall not bother to compare the liturgy of the Reformed churches today with Calvin's at this point, but if we did, it would soon be obvious that the central element of Calvin's view, the mystical union of the living Christ with his people, has completely dropped out. Let us, however, compare today's liturgy with the most truly Calvinist of the three theological standards, the Belgic Confession.

Article 35 of the Confession presents a very different theology from that of the liturgy. Christ is the heavenly bread coming down from heaven to be the true nourishment of the believer, who receives him by faith (the eyes and mouth of the soul) even as he eats the bread and drinks the wine. The background of this article is the whole imagery of John 6, which both Zwingli and the liturgy carefully reject. In fact, the Confession states that the godless receive the sacrament to their damnation, which is as nearly Lutheran as anything to be found in any Reformed Confession. No, the didactic portion explaining the meaning of the supper is as thoroughly anti-Calvinist and pro-Zwinglian as any Reformation document can be.

We should be grateful to the Württemberg Lutherans, for it is to them that we owe the last paragraph of the passage, the exhortation to true brotherly love among the communicants. The Palatinate form lifted this almost bodily from the Lutheran original, and we can be glad that it did.

Having been critical of the composition of the didactic part of the liturgy, let me say two things in praise of its communion prayer. As far as I know, it is the only communion prayer of the sixteenth century that brings out two elements strongly implicit in Calvin's eucharistic theology but nowhere expressed in Calvin's own liturgical forms.

The first is the Holy Spirit as the agent of the "miracle" (if that is the correct word) of the supper. Calvin never wearies in repeating that in the supper it is through the power of the Spirit that the living Christ is made present to the believer, whether, as he sometimes says, he is brought down or, as he elsewhere says, the congregation is lifted up. In either case, it is only the power of the Spirit that unites those who are separate.

Given the strong and constant emphasis on the presence of the Spirit in the supper in all of Calvin's writings about the supper, one would expect to find this faith expressed in Calvin's liturgy. Surprisingly enough the communion prayer contains not a word to this effect, nor does any liturgy of the Calvinistic family, except that of John Knox in Scotland. On the continent it is only our Palatinate-Dutch liturgy that contains a true epiclesis, invocation of the presence of the Spirit, in its liturgy for the supper.

The other noteworthy emphasis in this prayer, the work of the Palatine authors, is an eschatological one.

> And in all our suffering with uplifted head to look for the coming of our Lord Jesus Christ from heaven when he shall make our mortal bodies like unto his glorious body and take us to himself in eternity.

The eschatological side of the supper is an aspect that has come into consideration only very recently. How did it find its way into this liturgy back in the sixteenth century?

133

It would be comforting to think, as Lekkerkerker suggests, that the authors got their idea from a passage in Micron's *Christian Ordinances*. As part of the thanksgiving after communion in that form the minister says:

> I also hope that you who are sitting at the Table of the Lord have seen with the eye of faith that holy sitting together which is to come with Abraham, Isaac, and Jacob in the kingdom of God; and that you are certain of it through your faith in the righteousness, merit, and victory of Christ the Lord, just as we all have sat together at this table of the Lord.

There is certainly no similarity in language, but it is possible that Micron, whom the authors certainly knew, suggested the idea that they used in another way.

Beardslee makes an alternate suggestion, which I also find attractive. I have referred several times to the fact that, both in the Netherlands and in the Rhine Palatinate, the Reformed Church had, for a variety or reasons, attracted a number of right-wing Anabaptists, whose influence can never be forgotten. Beardslee feels that the inclusion of this eschatological passage, so atypical against the background of most Reformed liturgies, is one of their contributions to the Reformed liturgical tradition. In any event, I call your attention to the way in which both the short didactic passage and the communion prayer in our new liturgy have sought to emphasize this part of our heritage.

The remainder of the liturgy can be dealt with briefly. The final exhortation after the creed, "That we may now be fed with the true heavenly bread Christ Jesus, etc.," has been taken almost verbatim from Calvin, though the authors moderated somewhat the polemic quality of his language. (Incidentally, it is fairly obvious that it speaks a totally different view of the meaning of the supper from that contained in the longer didactic passage.)

I have already spoken about the words of distribution. Perhaps I need to say a word about the posture in receiving the supper. The custom of coming to sit at the table was, as far as I know, first used by à Lasco in London and has continued to be the custom of the Dutch church to this day. In other Reformed churches the custom is to stand around the table (German) or to kneel before it (French). It was Zwingli's custom to have the elements distributed to the congregation as they sat in their pews, a custom adopted by English Puritanism and finally in the late nineteenth century imitated by most Reformed congregations.

The liturgy concludes with a double thanksgiving, the reading of a part of Psalm 103 (with some additions) and a brief prayer. The prayer bears some resemblance to one in the Genevan liturgy and the theology is certainly Calvinist rather than Zwinglian. The interesting thing, however, is that in both the original Palatinate version and in Dathenus' translation the Psalm and the prayer are present as alternates. Between them very clearly are printed the words *or this.* Somewhere along the line the words "or this" were dropped out. Was this merely a printer's error or was it by deliberate design? We must leave the riddle unsolved.

*   *   *

This was the Sunday service that Reformed immigrants brought with them to the new world. In fact, nine years after its final revision by the Synod of Dort, it was used in a loft over a horse-mill in New Amsterdam for the first celebration of the Lord's supper in the Reformed Church. Doubtless, it was similarly used by van Raalte when the Lord's supper was first celebrated by his group of immigrants in western Michigan, for not even the great reorganization of the Dutch church in 1816 changed it. Its usage in North America and South Africa, long after it had fallen into disuse in the land of its birth and the land of its adoption, probably makes it the oldest Reformation liturgy continuously in use.

May I summarize its pedigree? The liturgy of the Dutch church was German in origin, composed of elements drawn from the liturgies of the French church in Strassburg, the Dutch church in London, the Lutheran church in Württemberg, woven together by a compiler whose theological cast was overwhelmingly Zwinglian.

But the story does not end there. Soon after its official adoption by the Dutch church, it was translated into English, and that started it on an entirely new career. Tracing the course of that career is another task.

VIII

CALVIN AND TOLERATION

PAUL WOOLLEY

We should begin by asking what it is that we are talking about. To look at the last part of our title first, we can find an element in the definition of "toleration" provided by the *Oxford English Dictionary* that appears to give us what we are looking for: "the action or practice of . . . allowing what is not actually approved; forbearance, sufferance." The last two terms appear to be primarily concerned with mental attitudes, while "allowing" may perhaps basically have a physical or legal, at least an external, reference. This definition, then, seems to me to embrace, in short compass, the varieties of attitude with which we are concerned. We want to find out about the

---

Paul Woolley teaches church history at Westminster Theological Seminary in Philadelphia. He received his academic training at Princeton University and Princeton Theological Seminary. He served as dean of the faculty of Westminster Theological Seminary, and as managing editor of the **Westminister Theological Journal** *from 1936 through 1967.*

mental climate as much as—perhaps more than—about the external permissions or prohibitions.

The other term of our subject is Calvin himself. I daresay that everyone at all acquainted with the Reformation has a mental image of Calvin. Confessedly it is not a perfect likeness. If, then, we freely seek more knowledge about him, it is well to question ourselves very briefly as to the atmosphere in which Calvin worked and as to the kind of man he was.

There were no century-old escutcheons in Calvin's family. His people had been plain bargemen on the French rivers. But the society in which they and he lived was still, in many respects, a feudal society. Sharp social distinctions he was used to. But superimposed on them were the distinctions of learning; and these he cherished, while he tolerated the others. He cherished them because he believed that they led to truth and, as the dedications of his books show, he endeavored to use the social distinctions to advance the distinctions of learning. Society had not easily lent itself to distinctions of learning. They inevitably, in view of the effects of sin on the mind of man, led to what the church called heresy, to what, on the standard of the word of God, often was heresy. The church had again refused, several centuries before Calvin was born, to be complacent about heresy, and into that lack of complacency he was born. The society in which Calvin lived was, then, much more a unitary one than ours.

But there were forces—primarily economic and religious—breaking that society apart. Calvin was himself a source of some of them, though it must be borne in mind that every force in a field is acted on, while it acts, by every other force, and that no one is free from the influence of the others. Calvin was influenced by Rome even while helping to counteract Rome.

Our subject, then, is toleration and Calvin, and we are talking about these in an historical context. What the uses of history may be is a lively topic today. The presses turn out book after book on the subject and the variety of approach is almost startling. In any case, one of the uses of history is not to encourage slavish imitation. This is neither desirable nor possible. Positively, one of the uses is surely to discover, in a situation of change affecting human life, the relative effects of the various forces that make for change and the powers that oppose it.

Calvin was a reformer. He provided a colossal amount of force to a movement that was disrupting the church of the day, radically altering its character. He succeeded in keeping the decrees of the Pope from having any force or effect within Geneva. The bishop's power was broken, the habits of the people were changed. They gave their children new names, they conducted business in a different way, they ate in novel restaurants, their entertainment was altered. Calvin was a reformer. Yet Calvin favored a capital sentence upon the heretic Servetus, he thought that witchcraft should be punished by the most severe penalty, he had exceedingly strict requirements for the ministers of Geneva, he favored a required subscription of belief from every inhabitant of the city, he wanted church attendance enforced by the civil magistrate. Calvin, say many moderns, was a tyrannical dictator. Here is a complex of forces that makes a study of Calvin and toleration something alive, something that encourages profound thinking.

Everyone has met individuals whose strong convictions lead them to live lives largely free of contact with other men. Calvin was not such a person. He had warm friends from his youth. He was an intimate of the Hangest family in his birthplace, Noyon. He held student office, annual deputy for the proctor of the Picard nation, while he was in the University of Orleans. He sought instruction from the best masters in Paris, whether they were congenial to the new learning or the old. Louis du Tillet became a close companion, to be succeeded later by Peter Viret and William Farel. With these men he either worked in physical proximity or carried on extensive correspondence. In

Strassburg he admired Martin Butzer and had many dealings with him and Wolfgang Capito. Before he left there he was working intimately with Luther's close follower, Philip Melanchthon, in endeavoring to negotiate an agreement with the theologians of Rome. Among a circle of such wide diversity Calvin found friends and congenial colaborers. He wrote to Melanchthon, "We may cheer each other with that blessed hope to which your letter calls us, that in heaven above we shall dwell forever, where we shall rejoice in love and in continuance of our friendship" (J. Bonnet [ed.], *Letters of John Calvin*, I, 374).

To Henry Bullinger, Zwingli's successor as the leader of the church in Zurich, Calvin wrote: "What ought we rather, dear Bullinger, to correspond about at this time than the preserving and confirming, by every possible means in our power, brotherly kindness among ourselves? . . . We must needs also endeavor by all means we can, that the churches to which we faithfully minister the word of the Lord may agree among themselves" (Bonnet, I, 113).

Calvin wished to live in an atmosphere of free intercourse and exchange of opinion even with those who held opinions fundamentally in opposition to his own. Speaking of those who differed with him about the Lord's supper, he said, "Were there any hope of mollifying these men, I would not refuse to humble myself, and by supplicating them, purchase the peace of the Church" ("Second Defense against Westphal," *Tracts and Treatises*, II, 248). And in his "Last Admonition to J. Westphal" he remarked, "I am not so given to avenge private injuries, as not to be ready, when any hope of cure appears, to lay aside all remembrance of them, and try all methods of brotherly pacification" (*Tracts and Treatises*, II, 348).

The Genevan Reformer wanted to use every possible means to advance agreement among group and organizations as well as among individuals. When Zurich theologians failed to attend a conference concerning Lutheran-Reformed agreement he wrote:

> We have reason to lament that good and otherwise right-hearted men are not more earnestly affected by the desire of promoting the public peace. For if they no longer need to care for the establishment among themselves of a godly union, they ought at least to consider it a duty to endeavor to come to a good mutual understanding with the churches. . . . If thus of set purpose we contend with each other, which can exceed the other in sin? (Bonnet, I, 89).

Calvin dedicated two commentaries to Edward VI, king of England, in order to advance the king's interest in the Reformation and to encourage him to consecrate "all to God and to our blessed Savior, who has so dearly purchased us. . . . I hope, indeed, sire, that God has stored you with such greatness and constancy of mind, that you will neither be weakened nor wearied. . . . Let me entreat you then, sire, to reach forward to the mark which is set before you."

Calvin did not object to dealing with any man or any organization, if the cause of truth might be forwarded thereby. The manner of carrying on the contest for truth was to be as all-embracing, as comprehensive, as the extent of mankind permitted. All men and all means were to be used toward that objective. Calvin wrote to Roman Catholics as well as to Protestants. He addressed Jacopo Sadoleto, the bishop of Carpentras, he addressed the Roman Catholic king of France, he addressed a personal friend who reverted to Rome, Louis du Tillet. To any man he was ready to extend an invitation to discussion. To any man he was prepared to say that he would make every effort within his power to discover truth, to bring others into agreement with it, to convince opponents of the true relationship that exists in this universe of God's creation. No trouble was too great to promote cooperation with others to the end of the triumph of God's cause.

Calvin's toleration toward persons was unlimited, unless he was convinced that those persons were firmly committed to making propaganda for error.

I have used the words "truth" and "error" in the preceding remarks. It seems impossible to picture Calvin without doing so. No delineation of Calvin would have any verisimilitude if it did not make a sharp distinction between truth and error. That distinction lay at the center of his thinking, as it still does at the heart of the thought of any man whose ideas can be safely used as guidelines for action.

What, then, can be said as to Calvin's views on tolerance in the realm of ideas, ideas concerning beliefs as to truth, ideas concerning procedures for action, ideas concerning established institutions and forms in society?

The most profitable way to enter into the heart of these matters will be to take each area by itself and endeavor to discover some of the things Calvin has said on the point. Especial attention will be paid to his comments on Scripture passages. Perhaps these are somewhat less well known than his other writings. They also have the advantage of allowing Calvin to speak in situations not immediately beclouded by the passion and prejudice of the contemporary Swiss, French, or German scene.

Calvin was thoroughly convinced that it was essential to distinguish truth from error. "Nothing is less tolerable than when God's truth is turned into a lie" (*Comm.* Ezek. 13:19). "It is therefore the duty of the Church to defend and publish the truth, that it may be honored by posterity from age to age" (*Comm.* Isa. 43:10). "Numerous scribblers arise . . . who not only obscure the light of sound doctrine with clouds of error . . . but by a profane license of skepticism, allow themselves to uproot the whole of Religion. . . . They have no axiom more plausible than, that faith must be free and unfettered, so that it may be possible, by reducing everything to a matter of doubt, to render Scripture flexible (so to speak) as a nose of wax. Therefore, they . . . obtain at length such proficiency, that they are always learning, yet never come to the knowledge of the truth" (*Comm.* Gen., I, liif.).

142

The need to preserve the truth is vital. "When Paul described it to be a quality which essentially belongs to faith—to know the truth, he plainly shows that there is no faith without knowledge" (*Comm.* Titus 1:1). "Away, then, with all errors and all wavering and doubtful opinions about God, if we wish to have experience of his favor!" (*Comm.* Isa. 43:14). "What they know is nothing, so long as they do not hold the truth, which is the foundation of all knowledge" (*Comm.* II Tim. 3:7).

There may, however, be differences of opinion as to what truth is. "Word has been brought me . . . that you [Christopher Libertet] did not entirely approve of some things in my treatise. . . . So far from being offended because of your opinion, I am greatly delighted with this straightforward plainness" (Bonnet, I, 43). But Calvin did not stop there. He wanted discussion of the differences so that truth might be elicited and clarified.

It may be necessary at times, Calvin felt, to defend the truth by conflict. "We are commanded to acquiesce in God's truth alone: but when a lie is offered to us instead of truth, what can we do but hesitate and at length engage in conflict? . . . Meanwhile, if the contention which we now perceive between those who boast themselves pastors of the Church disturbs us, let this example come to mind. . . . What we suffer the ancients have experienced" (*Comm.* Ezek. 13:2, 3). It is important not to allow ourselves to neglect this duty of defense. "No one ought to permit himself to be turned aside in different directions contrary to his conscience, because when he loses his free agency, he will be compelled to . . . obey the foulest commands" (*Comm.* Dan. 6:17).

The manner of defense is important: it must be Christian. "Some [ministers of the world] are always fulminating through a pretense of zeal, and forget themselves to be but men: they draw no sign of benevolence but indulge in mere bitterness. . . . Others, again, who are wicked and perfidious flatterers, gloss over the grossest iniquities"

143

(*Comm.* Dan. 4:20-22). "Thence it follows, that private persons would act improperly, and would be by no means countenanced by his [Moses'] example, if they sought to repress wrong by force and arms" (*Comm.* Ex. 2:12).

The magistrate, the state, however, Calvin took to be in a different position. He is under obligation to *repress* error. "God . . . will have us to restrain wickedness. To this end hath he appointed magistrates" (*Comm.* Acts 5:34). Does this, however, extend to error in idea, in concept? Calvin pointed out that the Donatists held that:

> no punishment ought to be inflicted on those who differ from others in religious doctrine. . . . What they desire is clear enough; . . . they wish to render everything uncertain in religion . . . and deny the right of inflicting punishment on heretics and blasphemers. . . . Augustine shows how ashamed Christian princes ought to be of their slothfulness, if they are indulgent to heretics and blasphemers, and do not vindicate God's glory by lawful punishments. . . . It follows that kings are bound to defend the worship of God, and to execute vengeance upon those who profanely despise it, and on those who endeavor . . . to adulterate the true doctrine by their errors (*Comm.* Dan. 4:1-3).

Such action on the part of the civil magistrate should be based on a clear understanding—and a presentation to the public—of the grounds for it. Nebuchadnezzar's edict prohibiting speech against the God of Shadrach, Meshach, and Abednego was "deserving of blame in this point, since he does not inquire what God's nature is, with the view of obtaining sufficient reason for issuing it" (*Comm.* Dan. 3:29). The magistrate has this immense authority only because he is God's representative. "This is the object of political government, that God's tribunal should be erected on earth, wherein He may exercise the judge's office, to the end that judges and magistrates should not . . . allow themselves to decide anything arbitrarily or wantonly, nor, in a word, assume to themselves what belongs to God" (*Comm.* Ex. 18:15).

144

Ignorance and weakness are, however, to be dealt with gently and kindly. "All teachers have . . . a rule here which they are to follow . . . modestly and kindly to accommodate themselves to the capacities of the ignorant and unlearned" (*Comm.* Rom. 1:14):

> This is what he [Isaiah] means by the metaphor of the bruised reed, that he does not wish to break off and altogether crush these who are half-broken, but, on the contrary, to lift up and support them, so as to maintain and strengthen all that is good in them (*Comm.* Isa. 42:3).
>
> We must neither crush the minds of the weak by excessive severity, nor encourage by our smooth language anything that is evil (*idem*).
>
> But these who boldly and obstinately resist . . . must be broken and crushed . . . by the severity of the word (*idem*).

This may take time, especially in the case of magistrates.

> Let us learn, therefore, from the Prophet's example, to pray for blessings on our enemies who desire to destroy us, and especially to pray for tyrants; . . . we must modestly bear their yoke because they could not be our governors without God's permission (*Comm.* Dan. 4:19).

The pastor, like the civil magistrate, must also defend the truth. "In a pastor there is demanded not only learning, but such zeal for pure doctrine as never to depart from it" (*Comm.* Titus 1:19). "A good pastor ought therefore to be on the watch, so as not to give silent permission to wicked and dangerous doctrines to make gradual progress, or to allow wicked men an opportunity of spreading them. . . . The Church may command them to be silent; and if they persevere, they may at least be banished from the society of believers, so that they shall have no opportunity of doing harm" (*Comm.* Titus 1:11). However, "the Church militant . . . has no permission to execute vengeance, except against those who obstinately refuse to be reclaimed" (*Comm.* Ps. 18:47).

145

It is clear that Calvin allows no tolerance for erroneous ideas if every opportunity has been given to correct them. Patience and charity are vital, for men are won to the right side by this method. But the time comes when stubbornness is not to be conquered and the magistrate must forcibly suppress error.

Can there be as broad a tolerance for action as for idea and concept? Calvin again and again speaks of the need for charity. "The object of this precept was to banish inhumanity and barbarism from the chosen people, and also to impress upon them horror even of a just execution" (*Comm.* Deut. 21:22f.). "Even philosophers look upon cruelty directed against the helpless and miserable, as an act worthy only of a cowardly and grovelling nature" (*Comm.* Ps. 109:16). Calvin suggests that the burning in the Israelite camp in the wilderness was kindled by God "in some extreme part, so as to awaken their terror, in order that there might be room for pardon" (*Comm.* Num. 11:1). There was room for pardon even when it might seem unlikely. "In the fact that a woman [Rahab] who had gained a shameful livelihood by prostitution was shortly after admitted into the body of the chosen people, and became a member of the Church, we are provided with a striking display of divine grace" (*Comm.* Josh. 2:1).

Right action is important, however. "It is accounted before God no less weighty a sin to violate His worship by gross and impure superstitions, than openly and professedly to fall away from religion altogether" (*Comm.* Deut. 17:2). Hypocrites are reminded "of the certainty of destruction should they longer presume upon the forbearance of God, and thus provoke his anger the more, by imagining that he can favor the practice of sin" (*Comm.* Ps. 50:21). All are reminded that "we . . . hold fast by this rule, that, in reference to things which are either commanded or forbidden of God, it is mainly requisite in the doing or forbearing that he may not be baulked of his due obedience, though we should offend the whole world"

(Bonnet, I, 303). "A servant knowing his master's will, and doing it not, is worthy of many stripes" (*Comm.* Amos 2:4f.).

There is, however, great latitude in many areas of conduct not prescribed by God's commandment. To a questioner in France he said, "the rule which I would propose for your observance, while you continue to live there, is that those [ceremonies] . . . which are not stamped with impiety you may observe, soberly indeed and sparingly, but when occasion requires freely and without anxiety. . . . Those which bear the smallest impress of sacrilege, you are no more to touch than you would the venom of a serpent" (*Tracts and Treatises,* III, 379). "Liberty lies in the conscience, and looks to God; the use of it lies in outward matters, and deals not with God only, but with men. . . . Liberty is not granted to the flesh, which ought rather to be held captive under the yoke, but is a spiritual benefit, which none but pious minds are capable of enjoying" (*Comm.* Gal. 5:13). So the effect of an action upon our fellow men is to be regarded. In his commentary on the remarks in I Corinthians 11:4 concerning covering the head, Calvin summarizes, "in fine, the *one* rule to be observed here is . . . decorum."

The created universe is always to be looked on as entrusted to man by God for proper use. Man is responsible for the performance of this trust. "Since then the wicked, by their perverse abuse of God's gifts, cause the world in a manner to degenerate and fall away from its first original, the prophet justly desires that they may be exterminated, until the race of them entirely fail" (*Comm.* Ps. 104:35). But this is not to be remembered unless there is also in mind the companion truth that "God's goodness, which thus contends with the wickedness of men, shines forth universally even towards the ungodly, so that He does not cease to cherish and preserve those whom He has created although they be unworthy" (*Comm.* Deut. 28:12). Commenting on Jeremiah 18:21, he says:

> The Prophet seems here to have been driven through indigna-
> tion to utter prayers which are not consistent with a right
> feeling; for even if Christ had not said with his own mouth,
> that we are to pray for those who curse us, the very law of
> God, ever known to the holy fathers, was sufficient. . . . But it
> must be observed that he was moved not otherwise than by
> the Holy Spirit to become thus indignant against his enemies;
> for he could not have been excused on the ground that
> indignation often transgresses the bounds of patience, for the
> children of God ought to bear all injuries to the utmost; but,
> as I have said, the Prophet here has announced nothing rash-
> ly, . . . but obediently proclaimed what the Holy Spirit dic-
> tated.

However, Calvin explains that "when God allures so gently
and kindly by his promises, and again pursues us with the
thunders of his curse, it is partly to render us inexcusable,
and partly to shut us up deprived of all confidence in our
own righteousness, so that we may learn to embrace his
covenant of Grace, and flee to Christ, who is the end of
the law" (*Commentary on the Four Last Books of Moses*,
I, xviii).

In sum, Calvin urges every effort to turn men to right
action. He points out that there is really a much greater
liberty of procedure than is often believed to be the case.
This must be recognized. Even when a man persists in what
is actually erroneous conduct, we must deal patiently with
him, if there is any hope of his turning from the wrong
ways. Only in the case of a stubborn and confirmed
transgressor should punishment finally be administered by
the magistrate. "He adds another exhortation, showing
how the faithful ought to act in reproving their brethren,
in order to restore them to the Lord. . . . To the meek and
teachable we ought to use kindness; but others, who are
hard and perverse, must be subdued by terror" (*Comm.*
Jude 22).

So far we have been thinking primarily in terms of
individuals. What was Calvin's attitude toward the institutions of his culture so far as they were involved in error?

He longed for the unity of the church, but he recognized that the errors and corruptions of Rome made it impossible to maintain such unity. He spoke of those who try to cover evil with good and "who imagine they can admirably adjust religious differences by simply adorning their too gross corruptions with attractive colors. The actual state of things compels them to confess that the vile errors and abuses of Popery have so far prevailed as to render a Reformation absolutely necessary" (*Comm.* Gen. 28:6). He spoke of the Pope as "that detestable monster, Antichrist, whose tyranny is exercised over the whole world" (*Comm.* Isa. 37:26). He saw the necessity of making the church worthy of confidence. "Nothing is more pestiferous in a Church than for men to be led away by a false confidence or trust" (*Comm.* Jer. 29:30-32). And he rejected the charge "that we have apostatized from the Church, because we have withdrawn from subjection to the See of Rome; . . . so Catholic—so universal—is the mass of errors by which they have overturned the whole of religion, that it would be enough to destroy and swallow up the Church a hundred times over" (*Comm.* John, I, 17). It was the leadership that was at fault. "We, indeed, Sadolet, deny not that those over which you preside are Churches of Christ, but we maintain that the Roman Pontiff, with his whole herd of pseudo-bishops . . . are ravening wolves" (*Tracts and Treatises,* I, 50).

The key to the desired unity of the church is the sole leadership of Christ. So Calvin even said that those "who at first extolled Henry [VIII], King of England, were certainly inconsiderate men; they gave him the supreme power in all things: and this always vexed me grievously; for they were guilty of blasphemy when they called him the chief Head of the Church under Christ" (*Comm.* Amos 7:10-13). But, further, Christ's truth was necessary to the unity. "I burned for the unity of thy Church, provided thy truth were made the bond of concord" (*Tracts and Treatises,* I, 60).

The unity of the church, then, must be built about the union of the body with the head. "Christ will not and cannot be torn from his Church with which he is joined in an indissoluble knot, as the head to the body. Hence unless we cultivate unity with the faithful, we see that we are cut off from Christ" (*Comm*. Ezek. 13:9). There is no use in expecting the earthly church to attain to perfection. Calvin remarks that "some leave the Church because they require in it the highest perfection. They are indignant at vices which they deem intolerable, when they cannot be corrected; and thus, under the pretext of zeal, they separate themselves and seek to form for themselves a new world, in which there is to be a perfect Church" (*Comm*. Hag. 2:1-5). Even though the officers are deficient, the church is still there:

> Whenever therefore it happens, by the Lord's permission, that the Church is administered by pastors, whatever kind of persons they may be, if we see there the marks of the Church, it will be better not to break the unity. Nor need it be any hindrance that some points of doctrine are not quite so pure, seeing that there is scarcely any church which does not retain some remnants of former ignorance. It is sufficient for us if the doctrine on which the Church of God is founded be recognized, and maintain its place (Bonnet, I, 101f.).

Calvin commended Butzer for not separating from Luther over what he called "trifling observances" (Bonnet, I, 137). He strove to prevent the schismatic division of "any Church whatsoever, which, however it might be very corrupt in morals, and infected with strange doctrine, had not cut itself off entirely from that doctrine, upon which Paul teaches the Church of Christ to be founded" (Bonnet, I, 117).

What was the doctrine on which the church of Christ was founded and what were "trifling observances"? To consider the latter first, there were observances that were not "trifling." The princes at Schmalkalden "displayed true greatness of soul" when they destroyed "certain impure images . . . together with their altars. They abolished also the elevation of the host in the supper" (Bonnet, I, 132). These non-trifling observances were to be eradicated. "Where there is the power of excommunication, there is an easy remedy for effecting a separation between the good and the bad" (*Comm.* I Cor. 5:10). When, therefore, the church has excommunicated anyone, no believer ought to receive him into terms of intimacy with himself" (*Comm.* I Cor. 5:11). However, there are limits here, as Calvin points out: "The Roman antichrist . . . has burst forth into interdicts, prohibiting anyone from helping one that has been excommunicated to food, or fuel, or drink, or any other supports of life. Now, that is not strictness of discipline, but tyrannical and barbarous cruelty."

The Reformation separation, then, was necessary. It is to be maintained by discipline and respected. "There are many proud men who despise the Church of God, because they think that God does not dwell in the midst of us, because we are obscure and of no great importance, and also because they regard our few number with contempt" (*Comm.* Hag. 2:1-5).

What now was the doctrine on which the church of Christ was founded? It was not something minor; it did not exclude differences of opinion. The church must continue, allowing freedom for variety of opinion. "We must not always reckon as contentious the man who does not acquiesce in our decisions, or who ventures to contradict us; but when temper and obstinacy show themselves, let us then say with Paul, that *contentions are at variance with the custom of the Church*" (*Comm.* I Cor. 11:16). "We must exercise moderation; so as not instantly to declare every man to be a 'heretic' who does not agree with our opinion. There are some matters on which Christians may differ from each other, without being divided into sects" (*Comm.* Titus 3:10). Even in Protestantism "overbearing tyranny has sprung forth already as the early blossom in the springtide of a reviving Church. . . . Let us therefore

151

... venture boldly to groan for freedom" (Bonnet, I, 467).

But how much freedom? Calvin suggests that the tests are "that the variety in the mode of teaching is such, that we all directed to one Christ, in whose truth being united together, we may grow up into one body and one spirit, and with the same mouth also proclaim whatever belongs to the sum of faith" (*Tracts and Treatises*, II, 34). He says, "If the whole aim of my vehemence was to prevent a good cause, even the sacred truth of Christ, from being overwhelmed ... why should it be imputed to me as a fault?" (*Tracts and Treatises*, II, 351). The test, then, is "the sacred truth of Christ," "the sum of faith." We shall return shortly to further consideration of these terms.

As already noted in another connection, the state has a duty, according to Calvin, with reference to the faith—the duty of being its protector. He reminded citizens that

> obedience is due to all who rule, because they have been raised to that honor not by chance, but by God's providence. For many are wont to inquire too scrupulously by what right power has been attained; but we ought to be satisfied with this alone, that power is possessed and exercised.... Subjects ought to obey their rules without hesitation.... There is no kind of government to which we ought not to submit.... There has never been a tyranny, nor can one be imagined, however cruel and unbridled, in which some portion of equity has not appeared (*Comm.* I Pet. 2:13f.).

On the other hand, rulers "are warned to submit reverently to God's Word and not to think themselves exempted from what is common to all, or absolved, on account of their dignity, for God has no respect of persons" (*Comm.* Jer. 36:29f.). Their duty is protection, not direction, of the church.

> What then is chiefly required of kings is this—to use the sword, with which they are invested, to render free ... the worship of God.... They are inconsiderate men who give them too much power in spiritual things.... We now find what fruit is pro-

duced by this root . . . princes think themselves so spiritual,
that there is no longer any church discipline; . . . they . . .
think that they cannot rule, except they . . . become chief
judges as well in doctrine as in all spiritual government
(*Comm.* Amos 7:10-13).

But when the church had established doctrine, the prince
might enforce it: "godly princes may lawfully issue edicts,
for *compelling* obstinate and rebellious persons to worship
the true God, and to maintain the unity of the faith; for,
though faith is voluntary, yet we see that such methods are
useful for subduing the obstinacy of those who will not
yield until they are compelled" (*Comm.* Luke 14:23). The
state for Calvin obviously occupied a much larger place in
matters of faith than is permitted by the Constitution of
the United States.

*   *   *

We have now perhaps reached the point where we may
cease to quote extensively from Calvin and may endeavor
to survey his position. To do so it is essential to think first
of the climate of opinion in which his ideas are developed.
The right of freedom of expression existed in a basic way
nowhere in western Europe. The papal inquisition was an
established institution except where the activity of the
Reformers had forced—temporarily, Rome hoped—a halt
(or where, in Spain, its powers had, in part, been absorbed
by the state). The physical cruelty that characterized the
Middle Ages had, as yet, seen little abatement. There were
no societies for the prevention of cruelty to children or to
animals. The civil magistrate everywhere assumed some
power to regulate the church, the degree differing most
frequently in inverse ratio to the power of the church in
that particular area but, in rare instances, also because of
the convictions of the ruler. It had long been assumed that
the criterion of heresy was the disapprobation of the Pope,

and inroads on that doctrine were only beginning to become established.

Against this background stands Calvin. His psychological attitude is basically a loving and kindly one. He wishes to promote an attitude of friendly brotherhood between the followers of Christ. There are, however, limits to this brotherhood, as is obvious from his characterization of the Pope as antichrist. It is not the type of brotherhood which allows equal standing to all ideas found to exist in the mind of a member of the human race. Instead, he makes a sharp distinction, unfashionable today, between truth and error. How does he recognize the two? This is a key question, but the answer is not hard to find. He has substituted the words of the Bible for the words of the Pope. The Bible is the only source of final authority.

Are brotherhood and friendliness interrupted, then, by divergence in opinions concerning truth? Not necessarily. Brotherhood is an important charge. It is a necessary consequence of common membership in the church, which is the body of Christ. Calvin was, as we have seen, even ready to recognize that there were congregations of the church of Christ in communion with Rome. But there were limits to the church. He found them not only in idea, in doctrine, but also in action, in practice. And, he said, they will be enforced by discipline in any true church.

In doctrine the church must teach Christ and his truth, "the sum of faith," or, as he put it elsewhere, "that doctrine upon which Paul teaches the Church of Christ to be founded" (Bonnet, I, 117). The limits here are nowhere marked out with a red pencil on a creed but they are not difficult to discover. They must not infringe upon the source of authority: witness Calvin's ultimate rejection of Castellio. They must not be anti-trinitarian: witness the rejection of Servetus. They must not impugn the efficacy of the finished work of Christ: witness his rejection of the Roman mass.

Right action is necessary to the recognition of a true

church. The sacraments are important. The strenuous efforts that culminated in the *Consensus Tigurinus* are witness to this. Calvin's signature of the *Augustana Variata* is also a witness, but it is likewise a witness as to the limits in the field of action. He would not sign the *Augustana Invariata* of 1530 but he could sign the *Variata* of 1540. The key lies in the difference between the two on the doctrine of the Lord's supper. His vigorous discussions with Joachim Westphal of Hamburg are evidence of the importance he attached to this area, the area of action.

If the variation in doctrine within the church passed the limits of "the sum of faith" or if the variation in action obscured the purpose of the sacrament or cast disrepute upon the church, it must protect itself, either by preventive action or by the exercise of discipline. There are numerous examples that might be cited. Perhaps we may take as an appropriate one the attitudes taken by Calvin towards other officers in Geneva.

After his first two years at Geneva, Calvin was banished from the city for insisting on maintaining the freedom of the church in the conduct of its own worship. His fellow-minister William Farel was expelled with him, and their successors were weak and flexible men. Yet from Strassburg Calvin insisted that these successors were appointed by the Lord and were worthy of honor and respect (Bonnet, I, 144). He cautioned the Genevans against any rebellion against them or failing to recognize them as spiritual parents.

A few years later, after Calvin had returned to Geneva, one of the teachers of the city, Sebastian Castellio, wished to become a minister. Calvin opposed his admission to the office on the ground of his opinions. Castellio's conclusion that the Song of Solomon was not properly a part of the canon of Scripture would be the occasion for trouble in the church, Calvin judged. Castellio also did not think that Calvin's interpretation of "he descended into hell" in the Apostles' Creed was a valid one. On these grounds he was

155

denied ordination to the ministry in Geneva, and the former of these two objections seems to have been the more powerful.

Here is an excellent example of the limits of Calvin's tolerance. He was charitable towards weakness, sympathetic towards good will and right intention. He could not, however, put his stamp of approval on a deletion from the Scriptures. This was undermining the basis on which the whole movement of Reform was founded. Personal feelings and conveniences were as nothing over against the welfare of the church. The healthy development of its members was the first charge. In studying Calvin one does not come to the conclusion, as is at times alleged, that he was an impersonal force, interested in an abstraction called truth. The welfare of the church consisted of the welfare of its members. What he was trying to do was to keep these sheep of Christ safe and to provide healthy conditions for their growth. This was his consuming desire and passion.

In great measure Calvin's desire was fulfilled. But it was fulfilled more fully and more acceptably abroad than in Geneva. The results of his work bore greater fruit in Scotland and in the Netherlands than they did in Switzerland. From both of these America ultimately benefited also. Does this result have any connection with the subject of toleration? Perhaps it does, since it is hardly likely that the ideas themselves had greater value for Scots and Netherlanders than for Genevans. While we cannot attempt here to prove this thesis, I am willing to say that, in my judgment, the greater fruitage of Calvin's ideas elsewhere than in Geneva is due to the fact that in other areas they were not subjected to implementation by the civil state to the same degree as was true in Geneva.

In Geneva the civil magistrate retained—in some instances temporarily and in some instances for longer periods—control over the selection of ministers, elders, and other church officers, over the imposition of disciplinary sanctions, over the forms for worship and administration of the sacraments, and over the religious conditions for citizenship. The doctrine and ethical principles of the church were incorporated into the civil code. Some of this was done against the wishes of Calvin, some of it with his thorough approval. It is here that his conception of toleration was not adequate.

The standard Calvin used, his measuring rod, the canon, was proper and perfect—the infallible Scriptures of the Old and New Testaments. His desire to see this canon recognized, applied, and implemented by every member of Christ's church was unimpeachably right. His personal love for the members of that church was warm, genuine, and catholic. He knew that its acceptance could only be effected by the Spirit of God moving in the individual heart.

It was, therefore, a lamentable mistake to allow the boundaries of error to be policed by civil servants and to be enforced by civil sanctions. A broader degree of civil tolerance would have complemented and adorned his personal virtue and have assisted in the attainment of an even wider scope for the insemination of those truths and principles he had so expertly developed from the conclusions of the earlier Reformers. He had purified them from dross, clarified them, and so cogently systematized them that their foundation in the Scriptures was patent and their delineation in the *Institutes of the Christian Religion* was a *chef d'oeuvre*. It is a *chef d'oeuvre* unsurpassed to the present day, which has enlightened and encouraged every generation of God's children during the tortuous course of these four intervening centuries.

IX

CALVINISM AND THE

AMERICAN REVOLUTION

CHARLES W. AKERS

In 1964 Professor Henry F. May of the University of California wrote in *The American Historical Review* that "for the study and understanding of American culture, the recovery of American religious history may well be the most important achievement of the last thirty years. A vast and crucial area of American experience has been rescued from neglect and misunderstanding. . . . Even for students of American culture who do not find religious thought and

―――――――――――――――――――――――――――――

Charles W. Akers received the Ph.D. degree from Boston University in 1952. He has been a professor at Eastern Nazarene College, Quincy Junior College, Geneva College, and Oakland University in Rochester, Michigan. From 1942 to 1946 he was a member of the United States Naval Reserve. Articles by Dr. Akers have appeared in **New England Quarterly, Mississippi Valley Historical Review,** *and* **Gavel.** *He is the author of* **Called Unto Liberty: A Life of Jonathan Mayhew.**

practice intrinsically interesting, knowledge of religious history has become a necessity."

For historians of the American colonies and Revolution, Professor May's statement has proved to be both a summary of past accomplishments and a signpost pointing to the future. I have noted with some excitement that a biography of John Winthrop, *The Puritan Dilemma* by Edmund S. Morgan of Yale University, is one of the most widely used volumes of collateral reading in college courses in American history. By examining in depth Winthrop's dilemma of how to do right while remaining in an evil society, Morgan has demonstrated the relevance of religious history and religious questions to American issues of today. But not even in the works of Becker, Beard, and Parrington of the Progressive generation was it possible to obscure completely the central role of religion in seventeenth-century America. Consequently, I find much more exciting the recent discovery by leading historians that the eighteenth century was such an intensely religious age that rather than describing the age through the lives of Franklin, Washington, and Jefferson, as we have often done, we must now seek to understand those men to some extent through a careful study of the religious currents of their times.

Here I must illustrate, even at the risk of being for a moment boringly bibliographical. Carl Bridenbaugh of Brown University, perhaps the most prolific colonial historian of this generation, concluded in a recent book that "no understanding of the eighteenth century is possible if we unconsciously omit, or consciously jam out, the religious theme just because our own milieu is secular." He added that "It is indeed high time that we repossess the important historical truth that religion was a fundamental cause of the American Revolution."

In an article written shortly before his untimely death in 1964, Perry Miller of Harvard, unquestionably the most important American intellectual historian and an avowed atheist, chided "obtuse" secularists such as Clinton Rossiter for regarding "religious utterances as being merely sanctimonious window dressing." The "reigning beliefs" of American society in 1776, Miller declared, "were still original sin and the need of grace." By concentrating on the rationalistic faith of Jefferson and Paine, scholars had missed "the basic fact . . . that the Revolution had been preached to the masses as a religious revival" and that "what aroused a Christian patriotism that needed staying power was a realization of the vengeance God denounced against the wicked; what fed their hopes was not what God promised as a recompense to virtue, but what dreary fortunes would overwhelm those who persisted in sloth; what kept them going was an assurance that by exerting themselves they were fighting for a victory thus providentially predestined."

In 1966 Miller's student Alan Heimert published a volume entitled *Religion and the American Mind from the Great Awakening to the Revolution*. This large book attempted to establish the thesis that the awakened, first-generation followers of Jonathan Edwards were the red hot revolutionaries of 1775. Heimert's study will be the subject of controversy for years to come, because he suggests that *The Life of . . . David Brainerd*, Edwards' most popular work, is as important a key to "the eighteenth-century temper" as Franklin's *Autobiography;* that the colonial reaction to the death of George Whitefield in 1770 at Newburyport, Massachusetts, contributed as much fervor to the Revolutionary movement as did the Boston Massacre of the same year; that Jefferson will have to share honors as the foremost champion of religious freedom with Isaac Backus, the leader of New England Separate Baptists; that July 20, 1775, Congress Sunday (the national day of prayer throughout the colonies), deserves to be celebrated fully as much as July 4, 1776; that Nathaniel Whitaker, a Calvinist pastor of Salem, was "the first orator of American Democracy," surely more influential than

James Otis and Patrick Henry; and that Edwards' *Freedom of the Will* (1754) "was actually the Calvinist handbook of the Revolution." Although Heimert has greatly exaggerated his thesis, much of the evidence he has uncovered will in my judgment stand the test of historical investigation.

Heimert's study points once again to the necessity and difficulty of interpreting Jonathan Edwards, who, since Perry Miller's biography, has become the dominant intellectual figure of the colonial period. In sharp contrast to Heimert is a book by James P. Carse of New York University, *Jonathan Edwards and the Visibility of God*. Carse contends that neither Edwards nor his writings played any significant part in the shaping of the republic that emerged from the Revolution. Instead, the failure of Edwards was the miscarriage of our developing civilization. After him "every great American prophet would fail in the same way," because Americans refuse to join profession of the Christian faith with the practice of it. In other words, as Carse puts it, our journey toward the "ultimate society" ended in 1750 when the Northampton congregation rejected the pastor who demanded that they make God visible in their lives. If I read Carse correctly—and I am not at all sure I do—the New Left has discovered Jonathan Edwards. One can be certain that we have not seen the last new interpretation of this frontier genius.

Edmund S. Morgan is currently devoting ten years of his career to a full study of the place of the Puritan ethic in American civilization. By the Puritan ethic he means those "values, ideas, and attitudes" that cluster around the Protestant doctrine of the calling as it was stressed by the Calvinists and Lutherans who settled America. Already he has published an article in which he maintains that "patriotism and the Puritan Ethic marched hand in hand from 1764 to 1789." For example, he sees a major division in the Continental Congress between those men who made the Puritan ethic only a matter of faith and not practice and those who both believed it and sought to exemplify it in daily living. Likewise, the split between Samuel Adams and John Hancock in Massachusetts after 1777 can be explained to a considerable extent by the refusal of Hancock to put aside the worldly pleasures and luxuries so despised by Adams.

Some historians have not yet recovered from the shock they received in 1966 when a book entitled *Isaac Backus and the American Pietistic Tradition*, by William G. McLoughlin of Brown University, made its appearance in the popular "Library of American Biography" series, which has for the most part been devoted to such standard notables as Daniel Webster, Henry Clay, Woodrow Wilson, and Eli Whitney. Who is Isaac Backus? The answer—leader of the New England Separate Baptists—does not shed much light on him, because few can identify the Separate Baptists. But as the leader of the most protracted, vigorous, and successful campaign for separation of church and state in America, Backus can no longer be ignored. Unlike Jefferson and Madison, "Backus and the Baptists wanted to separate Church and State in order to create a truly Christian state in which men rendered to Caesar only what was really Caesar's and devoted the bulk of their energy to serving God." McLoughlin reminds us that it was Backus' version of separation that won the day with "a nation of pietists" and that only in the recent twentieth century has there been a swing to the secular version of Jefferson and Madison.

To mention briefly only one more recent study of the role of religion in the eighteenth century, Richard L. Bushman's *From Puritan to Yankee, Character and the Social Order in Connecticut, 1690-1765*, published in 1967, does a remarkable job of demonstrating that religious and economic forces were almost equally responsible for the shaping of the pre-Revolutionary social order of Connecticut.

Why such a new awareness of religious forces in American history generally and the Revolutionary era particularly? It is largely the result of a new look at the evidence from the point of view that the documents should be sampled accurately. Quantitatively, religious concerns have always occupied a significant share of the time and energies of Americans. Only by deciding in advance that the vast documentation for religious influences was unimportant did the historical profession reach the point that in 1922 Harold Stearns could explain that "there was no article on religion in his *Civilization in the United States*" because he could find no competent historian interested in writing it.

While preparing studies of two New England preachers of the eighteenth century, I have been amazed to discover the existence of seemingly endless evidence that "the Spirit of '76," although a mixture of many elements, had a marked religious tone. It is apparent that not only were there conspicuous religious elements in the overt causal pattern of the Revolution, but that in subtle ways religion shaped the American response to British measures, influenced the relation of the rank and file to their leaders during the war, helped to turn a civil clash over imperial issues into a holy crusade against the evil power of Britain, and in the moment of victory made a spiritual interpretation of the Revolution almost irresistible not only to the orthodox but also to such erstwhile skeptics as Benjamin Franklin.

I plan to develop these themes in a book to be published by Harcourt, Brace and World as a volume in their series to commemorate the bicentennial of the Revolution. Already, however, I am aware that I face an endless task. Should I read all of the documentation easily available, the book would more likely be published in 2076 than in 1976. In this paper I should like to share a few samples of this evidence and then suggest how the return to the evidence may possibly influence historical interpretation of the Revolution.

In 1774, the British government, following a divide-and-rule policy, decided to punish Massachusetts for its rebelliousness but for the time being to take no action against the other colonies. Among other measures the Boston Port Bill would shut that port on June 1, 1774, until Boston paid for the tea destroyed the previous year. When Thomas Jefferson and a few other members of the Virginia House heard the news, they resolved to initiate some step to demonstrate that Virginia stood firm with Massachusetts. Jefferson describes their plan in his *Autobiography:*

> We were under conviction of the necessity of arousing our people from the lethargy into which they had fallen, as to passing events; and thought that the appointment of a day of general fasting and prayer would be most likely to call up and alarm their attention. No example of such a solemnity had existed since the days of our distresses in the war of '55, since which a new generation had grown up. With the help of Rushworth [a historical work], whom we rummaged over for the revolutionary precedents and forms of the Puritans of that day, preserved by him, we cooked up a resolution, somewhat modernizing their phrases, for appointing the 1st day of June, on which the portbill was to commence, for a day of fasting, humiliation, and prayer, to implore Heaven to avert from us the evils of civil war, to inspire us with firmness in support of our rights, and to turn the hearts of the King and Parliament to moderation and justice. To give greater emphasis to our proposition, we agreed to wait the next morning on Mr. Nicholas, whose grave and religious character was more in unison with the tone of our resolution, and to solicit him to move it. We accordingly went to him in the morning. He moved it the same day; the first of June was proposed; and it passed without opposition. The Governor dissolved us, as usual. . . . We returned home, and in our several counties invited the clergy to meet assemblies of people on the 1st of June, to perform the ceremonies of the day, and to address to them discourses suited to the occasion. The people met generally, with anxiety and alarm in their countenances, and the effect of the day, through the whole colony, was like a shock of electricity, arousing every man, and placing him erect and solidly on his centre.

Even if he was using this religious appeal only for

propaganda purposes, Jefferson knew the people of Virginia. In his *Notes on Virginia* he estimated that by 1776 two-thirds of the inhabitants of this colony, where the Church of England was established by law, were, nevertheless, dissenters. In Virginia, as elsewhere in the colonies, the vast majority of the people came from a radical dissenting tradition and at least a bare majority were Calvinists who gave allegiance to the Westminster Confession. As a result, the day of prayer, fasting, and humiliation could become an effective instrument for uniting Christian hearts in a common cause. Although used by every colony and by the Continental Congress for all the colonies, this instrument has remained largely unstudied. The proclamations calling the people to prayer would fill a large book. Such a volume would tell as much concerning the state of the nation being formed as any collection of political or economic documents. Here, for example, is the resolution of the Congress passed in the fall of 1777 after the seemingly miraculous victory at Saratoga:

> Forasmuch as it is the indispensible Duty of all Men, to adore the superintending Providence of Almighty God:—To acknowledge with Gratitude their Obligation to Him for Benefits receivd, and to implore such further Blessings as they stand in Need of:—And, it having pleased Him in his abundant Mercy, not only to continue to us the innumerable Bounties of His common Providence; but also to smile upon us in the Prosecution of a just and necessary War for the Defence and Establishment of our unalienable Rights and Liberties. Particularly in that He hath been pleased, in so great a Measure to prosper the Means used for the Support of our Troops, and to crown our Arms with most signal Success.
>
> It is therefore recommended to the Legislative or Executive Powers of these United States, to set apart Thursday the Eighteenth of December, next, for solemn Thanksgiving and Praise. That at one Time, and with one Voice, the good People may express the grateful Feelings of their Hearts, and consecrate themselves to the Service of their divine Benefactor. And, that together with their sincere Acknowledgments and Offerings, they may joyn the penitent Confession of their

165

manifold Sins, whereby they had forfeited every Favor; and their humble & earnest Supplication that it may please God through the Merits of Jesus Christ mercifully to forgive and blot them out of Remembrance. That it may please Him, graciously to afford His Blessing on the Governments of these States respectively, and prosper the publick Council of the whole. To inspire our Commanders both by Land and Sea, & all under them with that Wisdom and Fortitude which may render them fit Instruments, under the Providence of Almighty God, to secure for these United States, the greatest of all human Blessings, *Independence* and *Peace*. That it may please Him, to prosper the Trade and Manufactures of the People, and the Labor of the Husbandman, that our Land may yet yield its Increase. To take Schools and Seminaries of Education, so necessary for cultivating the Principles of true Liberty, Virtue, & Piety, under His nurturing Hand; and to prosper the Means of Religion for the Promotion and Enlargement of that Kingdom which consisteth "in *Righteousness Peace and Joy in the Holy Ghost.*"

And it is further recommended, that servile Labor, and such Recreation as, though at other times innocent, may be unbecoming the Purpose of this Appointment, may be omitted on so solemn an occasion.

As Perry Miller expressed it so well, this fusion of Calvinistic theology, radical Whig political theory, and colonial tradition became "a dynamo for generating action."

The sermons preached during the Revolution are the best-known source on its religious dimension. On the eve of the Civil War two anthologies of Revolutionary sermons and a book on the clergy who preached them were published, as the preface on one stated, to remind the nation in its current crisis of "the secret of that moral energy which sustained the Republic in its material weakness against superior numbers, and discipline, and all the power of England." Historians have quoted frequently from these anthologies and a few other well-known titles, but most of the sermons had remained unstudied until Heimert did his work. His radical conclusions, derived almost entirely from this source, indicate the potential of a continued study of the sermons. The Evans *Bibliography* lists 338 printed sermons for the years 1774 to 1783, and many hundreds more are extant in manuscript. A few excerpts will illustrate what Miller meant when he declared "that the Revolution had been preached to the masses as a religious revival."

John Lathrop, 1770:

> Genesis iv:10. . . . the voice of thy brother's blood crieth unto me from the ground.
>
> I need not inform you, my hearers, that the bloody and most cruel action of last Monday evening [Boston Massacre] led me to the choice of the words which have now been read for the subject of the following discourse. We should be criminal to let such an awful affair pass over without taking notice of it in a religious manner.
>
> The unparalleled barbarity of those who were lately guilty of murdering a number of our innocent fellow citizens will never be forgot. . . . Future generations will read the account with sorrow, indignation, and surprise: sorrow for the dead who fell victims to the devilish rage of wicked men; indignation against the worst of murderers; and surprise that any rational beings could be so destitute of every humane feeling as wantonly to destroy those who never did or thought of doing them any hurt.

Samuel Williams, 1774:

> As what should further confirm our attachment to our native country, it bids fairest of any to promote the perfection and happiness of mankind. We have but few principles from which we can argue with certainty, what will be the state of mankind in future ages. But if we may judge the designs of providence, by the number and power of the causes that are already at work, we shall be led to think that the perfection and happiness of mankind is to be carried further in America, than it has ever yet been in any place.

William Smith, 1775:

> Illiberal or mistaken plans of policy may distress us for a

167

while, and perhaps sorely check our growth; but if we maintain our own virtue; if we cultivate the spirit of liberty among our children; if we guard against the snares of luxury, venality and corruption; the Genius of America will still rise triumphant, and that with a power at last too mighty for opposition. This country will be free—nay for ages to come a chosen seat of Freedom, Arts, and Heavenly Knowledge; which are now either drooping or dead in those countries of the old world.

Samuel Cooper, 1780:

Peace, peace, we ardently wish; but not upon terms dishonorable to ourselves, or dangerous to our liberties; and our enemies seem not yet prepared to allow it upon any other. At present the voice of Providence, the call of our still invaded country, and the cry of everything dear to us, all unite to rouse us to prosecute the war with redoubled vigor.

Ezra Stiles, 1783:

. . . Congress put at the head of this spirited army the only man [Washington] on whom the eyes of all Israel were placed. Posterity, I apprehend, and the world itself, inconsiderate and incredulous as they may be of the dominion of Heaven, will yet do so much justice to the divine moral government as to acknowledge that this American Joshua was raised up by God, and divinely formed, by a peculiar influence of the Sovereign of the universe, for the great work of leading the armies of this American Joseph (now separated from his brethren), and conducting this people through the severe, the arduous conflict, to liberty and independence.

After reading a few of these addresses from the pulpit, one begins to understand why General Frederick Haldiman, the French-speaking officer who was second in command to Gage in Boston, 1774-1775, noted in his diary that the Congregational clergy of New England "are the most dangerous of all beings"; why a British major told the pious patriot prisoners he was guarding during the siege of Boston, "It is your G-d Damned Religion of this Country that ruins the Country; Damn your religion"; and why American loyalists cursed the "black regiment" of dissenting clergymen who "unceasingly" sounded "the Yell of Rebellion in the Ears of an ignorant & deluded People."

The most neglected source on the religious tone of the Revolution is the newspaper. I am convinced that very few scholars have read all the newspapers published during the Revolution, as I am now attempting to do. The quantity of evidence available in this source is staggering. Two examples will have to suffice here.

In the fall of 1777, as Burgoyne led his army south from Canada to join Clinton and crush the rebellion, the *Boston Gazette*, most radical of patriot newspapers—"the weekly dung barge," as Tories called it—gave its front page for three consecutive issues to a fast sermon preached some time earlier. I doubt that there was a clearer, more effective statement of how American patriots understood the issues of the Revolution. The text was II Chronicles 20:11-12: "Behold how they reward us, to come to cast us out of thy Possession, which thou hast given us to inherit. O our God, wilt thou not judge them? For we have no might against this great company that cometh against us: neither know we what to do, but our eyes are upon thee." The outline could not be clearer:

I. That this our land is God's possession, which He has given us to inherit.
II. That no other man, or body of men, have a right to this possession, or any part of it, unless we see cause to give it to him, or them, for some good or valuable consideration; and therefore,
III. Great Britain in sending an army to turn us out of our possession, merely because we will not resign up ourselves and property, to be disposed of at her will and discretion, is unjust and barbarous; and therefore,
IV. As this army is come against us, and as we cannot trust in an arm of flesh, or upon our counsel alone, we ought to have our eyes upon God, for him to espouse our cause, and put an end to the quarrel.

169

And finally, the theory stated, came the injunction to fight:

> When God, in his providence, calls to take the sword; if any refuse to obey, Heaven's dread artillery is levelled against him, as you may see, Jer. 48.10. Cursed be he that keepeth Back His Sword from blood; cursed is that sneaking coward who neglects the sinking state, when called to its defence—O then, flee this dire curse.

Another newspaper proclaimed the same message more succinctly: "Thus saith the Lord, shake off the yoke of Albion and the king therof, and chuse unto yourself judges and rulers out of your own tribe to govern you."

Among many other points, one can demonstrate from newspaper evidence that the colonists retained a lively interest in theological issues while prosecuting the war. I cite the following verses more for interest than importance. In the *Continental Journal* for March 11, 1779, appeared these lines entitled "On Predestination":

> If all things succeed as already agreed,
>   And immutable impulses rule us;
> To preach and to pray, is but time thrown away,
>   And our teachers do nothing but fool us.
>
> If we're driven by fate, either this way or that,
>   As the carman whips us his horses,
> Then no man can stray—all go the right way,
>   As the stars that are fix'd in their courses.
>
> But if by free will, we can go or stand still,
>   As best suits the present occasion;
> Then fill up the glass, and confirm him an ass
>   That depends upon Predestination.

The inevitable answer appeared two weeks later in the same newspaper:

> If an all perfect mind rules over mankind,

With infinite wisdom and power;
Sure he may decree, and yet the will be free,
 The deeds and events of each hour.

If scripture affirms in the plainest of terms,
 The doctrine of Predestination;
We ought to believe it, and humbly receive it,
 As a truth of divine revelation.

If all things advance with the force of meer chance,
 Or by human free will are directed;
To preach and to pray, will be time thrown away,
 Our teachers may be well rejected.

If men are deprav'd, and to vice so enslav'd,
 That the heart chuses nothing but evil;
Then who goes on still by his own corrupt will,
 Is driving post haste to the devil.

Then let human pride and vain cavil subside,
 It is plain to a full demonstration,
That he's a wild ass, who over his glass,
 Dares ridicule Predestination.

As plentiful as is the newspaper evidence, the historian who wishes to recover the full religious thrust of the Revolution must turn to the manuscripts left by the men and women who experienced that long war between 1775 and 1781. Here we discover that a natural concentration by historians of the past on the major leaders of the Revolution, most of whom were scandalously unorthodox in religion, has obscured the piety and orthodoxy of the secondary leaders and the rank and file. For 175 years we have attempted to make George Washington into an evangelical Christian because we think the father of a Christian country should have been saintly. Washington's death in 1800 was lamented by the clergy of the nation as the loss of a leader so godly that he had seemingly spent as much time during the war praying and inculcating morality in his troops as in fighting the Redcoats. Mason L. Weems put the finishing touches on the image a few years later by escorting Washington into heaven at the end of a biography which permanently enshrined the myth already created. Not long ago Billy Graham described on coast-to-coast television his visit to the spot at Valley Forge where Washington had knelt in prayer, a scene which earlier had been commemorated on our two-cent postage stamp. I hope that Paul L. Boller has forever put an end to such nonsense with his book, *George Washington and Religion*. He shows that it is impossible to identify the adult Washington in any positive way as a Christian. Like Jefferson, John Adams, and Benjamin Franklin, any trace of evangelical orthodoxy in his life was a reflection of the society in which he lived.

Although a full study of the religion of the secondary national leaders and local leaders of the Revolution is yet to be made, the evidence suggests that the majority were as orthodox as the nation at large. General John Sullivan, who preached the message of American righteousness to the British general opposing him in Rhode Island, appears far more typical of patriot military leaders than the commander-in-chief. The effectiveness of Samuel Adams in arousing patriotic fervor can be attributed in part to his speaking sincerely the religious idiom of his fellow countrymen. When he repulsed the British commissioners of reconciliation in 1778 with the words, "We again make our solemn appeal to the God of heaven to decide between you and us," he spoke the sentiments of a people who had suffered through three years of war but who were determined to fight on in a righteous struggle rather than compromise with sin. All war is an appeal to heaven, as Locke pointed out and as the flag of the Boston *Independent Chronicle* reminded its readers weekly for several years during the Revolution. Many American patriots made this appeal with confidence "that God fights for America," as Noah Welles phrased it, and thus the British dependence on "an arm of flesh" was doomed to fail against the heavenly forces enlisted in the colonial cause. Seen in this perspective, "Christian retaliation" against British "atrocities," persecution of the loyalists, and even alliance with popish France appeared justifiable and natural.

In the light of present knowledge, it is difficult to explain the paradox of revolutionary leadership: how could a nation of orthodox Christians be led into war by near-Deists? My tentative conclusion is that the atheological, moralistic religion of the top men made them more effective leaders by reducing the doctrinal barriers between them and their followers. It is important here to know more about the deification of Washington. At the end of the war one anonymous newspaper correspondent wrote that Washington's circular letter to the states "was dictated by the immediate Spirit of God"—hardly a statement that a zealous Calvinist could have made concerning the writing of an equally zealous Arminian. A fuller and more satisfactory explanation of the paradox must await the complete exploration of the relation of revolutionary leaders to their constituents.

*   *   *

It is likely that during the approaching bicentennial the multitude of young scholars now beginning to work in this field will provide the evidence necessary for the first adequate analysis of the role of religion in the Revolution. Already the work done has partially restored the religious idiom in which the American revolutionaries articulated their war aims and enjoined their brethren to fight on. And there is a new awareness that this language was often not so much propaganda as the sincere expression of a people who would not have understood our modern notion that one can hold his religious values apart from his political and economic views.

As this research proceeds, we shall have to add new

names to the pantheon of important revolutionaries, names such as Isaac Backus, John Witherspoon, Joseph Hawley, Nathaniel Whitaker, and many others. In this pantheon I hope to erect the bust of Samuel Cooper, Calvinist minister of the Brattle Street Church of Boston. Under a cloak of clerical anonymity Cooper did almost as much as Samuel Adams to foment rebellion and see it through to victory. The greatest Boston orator of his day, pastor to Hancock, Bowdoin, and at times to John Adams, confidant of Benjamin Franklin, "Silver-tongued Sam" won Lafayette's praise as the foremost American supporter of the French alliance. By his death just after the peace treaty, he was the acknowledged *de facto* "prime minister" to Governor Hancock. He may indeed have been the major influence on Hancock's entire revolutionary career.

A further product of the new research may be answers to some important questions that have puzzled students of the Revolution. To focus on only one, why was the radical Whig political philosophy of Milton, Sidney, and Locke that was so readably summarized in *Cato's Letters*, widely accepted in the colonies but scorned as the product of a lunatic fringe in the mother country? It would appear that in America this philosophy found the spiritual and environmental support it lacked in England. Before the bicentennial observances are concluded, I expect to see a book by some eager young Ph.D. telling us what every eighteenth-century Calvinist knew—that the Bible was the primary source of his political concepts and that the radical Whig philosophy was acceptable because it was first compatible with Holy Writ and then also proved useful in defending the claims of colonial assemblies to legislative supremacy within their respective colonies.

Since Thomas Paine wrote in the last *Crisis* paper, "The times that try men's souls are over, and the greatest and completest revolution the world ever knew is gloriously and happily accomplished," men have debated the meaning of the Revolution. Through the centennial edition of Bancroft's *History* in 1876, American historians recognized that the Revolution had a deep spiritual significance, but until recently in the twentieth century only foreign students of American civilization have preserved the insight that our national birth was a spiritual as well as political trauma. By leaping from the question of why we broke with Britain to the conclusion that the adoption of the Constitution was the real meaning of the struggle, our historians failed to notice the way in which fighting a long war against what seemed like impossible odds modified American values and attitudes and contributed to the creation of a new nationalism. After a few months of bloodshed Abigail Adams could write that "Our Country is as it were a Secondary God" which should take precedence over all except God himself. As we ponder the meaning of the American Revolution in full knowledge of its religious dimension, we shall have to face some hard questions. Perhaps the most important of these is to what extent a triumphant, religiously shaped nationalism that permitted the substitution of political for religious orthodoxy permanently fixed the course of the United States away from John Winthrop's "City upon a Hill" toward Harvey Cox's "secular city." Perhaps by 1976 we shall be sufficiently mature as a nation to raise the question of what we lost as well as gained by the Revolution.

Preparations for the celebration of 1976 are now under way. As we plan it is important to recall that the observances of 1876 appear to have been of little consequence, indeed, often silly from our present vantage point. Some Americans wrote books, poems, or articles of no lasting value or visited the Philadelphia Centennial Exposition to see exhibits illustrating our burgeoning industrial and technological power. Others planted liberty trees, a few of which still survive. But most seem to have displayed their patriotism only by getting drunk on July 4, 1876, while they listened to the bombastic oratory of local politicians who were careful to confirm the prejudices of the electorate. A major Detroit newspaper proposed that the entire celebration be called off on the ground that the citizens of Michigan needed no additional excuse for drunkenness. It is difficult to find in the record of the centennial any concerted effort to bring about a reappraisal of the national purpose and direction.

It is my hope that the recovery of the knowledge that the American Revolution had a significant religious character will do more than set straight the historical record; that this knowledge will stimulate us to use the occasion of 1976 for more serious and meaningful observances and reflections than in 1876; that it will remind us again that many of the hard questions we must face concerning our national existence are, as they were in 1776, ultimately religious questions.

X

CALVINISM AND DEMOCRACY

ROBERT M. KINGDON

The man who founded "Congregationalism" in France, perhaps in the entire Christian world, was Jean Morely, sire de Villiers. He came from a petty noble family headquartered in central France, near Paris. His father may have

Robert M. Kingdon received his academic training at Oberlin College, the University of Geneva (Switzerland), and Columbia University. In 1960-61 he conducted research in Europe as a Fellow of the American Council of Learned Societies, and in 1966-66 he conducted research in Princeton, New Jersey, as a member of the Institute for Advanced Study. He has taught at the University of Iowa, Amherst College, Stanford University, and the University of Wisconsin. He is the author of **Geneva and the Coming of the Wars of Religion in France 1555-1563** *and* **Geneva and the Consolidation of the French Protestant Movement 1564-1572,** *and he collaborated with J. F. Bergier and A. Dufour in the publication of* **Registres de la Compagnie des Pasteurs de Geneve au temps de Calvin.**

been a physician, perhaps even attached to the royal court. His writing makes it clear that he acquired a modest education, including Latin and a little Greek; thorough acquaintance with the Bible, with some of the church fathers, and with such pagan authorities as Aristotle; and finally a solid knowledge of Calvin's theology. In 1554, driven probably partly by persecution, attracted probably partly by the excitement of the great Calvinist experiment, he moved to Geneva. There he developed close friendships with other French refugee nobles. He came to know Calvin personally. And he came to know a fellow noble refugee who was to become his most implacable opponent within the Calvinist movement, Theodore Beza.

It was also in Geneva that Morely worked out his new theory of church government. He presented it first to Calvin, in the form of a bulky manuscript, but Calvin was preoccupied at the time with directing a feverish missionary campaign that was reaching its peak within France, and was too busy to read it. Soon thereafter Morely moved to Lyon, at about the time this great French commercial and financial center became temporarily Calvinist, won over to the Reformed faith by the fiery preaching of Pierre Viret. Here Morely presented his manuscript to Viret, who leafed through it hastily, but could not find time to study it with care. Morely arranged with the great printer de Tournes to publish it, and it appeared in 1562 under the title *Traicté de la discipline & police Chrestienne*. Dedicated to Viret and presented to the next National Synod of the French Reformed Church, it immediately created a furor.

The reasons for this furor can best be discovered by direct analysis of this revolutionary little book. These reasons are not to be found, however, in its basic premises. For these premises are simple propositions typical of most Calvinist thought of that period. Calvin himself, furthermore, is quoted with respect in the book. And the fundamental Calvinism of Morely's theological position becomes even clearer in the controversy following release of his book. When at one point he was challenged on his ideas of predestination, for example, he wrote out in his own hand a summary statement of his views on this particularly controversial dogma, a statement which then, as now, would have to be accepted as unexceptionably orthodox Calvinism. Indeed the basic concern that led to the writing of this book was characteristic of much early Calvinism: concern over the problem of *discipline*—as it was then called—the problem of how erroneous belief and delinquent behavior can be ferreted out and punished. This was the problem the highly controversial Genevan Consistory had been created to solve. It was the problem that had provoked the departure of Viret and other loyal disciples of Calvin from Lausanne and the other French-speaking cities controlled by the mighty Swiss Republic of Berne. It was the problem that was later to provoke the entire Erastian controversy, which upset the Reformed community in Germany, in Switzerland, and in England.

As Morely studied this discipline problem, however, he reached a conclusion quite different from that of Erastus or Beza. He became convinced that it could only be solved by action of an entire local congregation. It is, he felt, a problem creating responsibilities which should not be delegated to any special institutions or church officers, but which should rather be shouldered by every member of every church. A sinner's actual neighbors are those best placed to discover waywardness and to admonish him. And if more serious punishments such as excommunication prove necessary, they too should be leveled only by the entire local body of believers. Morely considered this solution to the discipline problem to be dictated by the New Testament and by practical considerations alike. He granted that a few particularly difficult and complex disciplinary cases might be referred to ecclesiastical bodies of great generality which were representative in character, specifically to provincial and national synods. But he remained quite suspicious of such bodies, and at one point even

179

went so far as to charge some of the early ecumenical councils with having fomented error. Obviously he wanted to restrict considerably the powers of such representative bodies.

In developing his argument further, Morely next turned to the problem of selecting clergymen. Here again he argued for what we would call "congregationalism." He felt that every variety of minister then provided for by Calvinist polity, particularly pastors and elders, should be selected by methods providing more voice to the entire local congregation to be served. Not only should ministers be selected by the local congregations; they should also be subject to dismissal by the flocks they served. Morely's proposed procedures contrasted significantly with those in actual use among most contemporary Calvinist churches, at least in the larger communities of Switzerland and France. Faced with a vacancy in the ranks, the body of ministers in a Reformed community surveyed appropriate candidates as a "company," and selected, as a "company," those whose training, beliefs, and personal qualifications best fitted them for the positions open. Entire congregations were consulted only at a fairly late stage in this process. They were allowed to hear nominees proposed by the general "company" of pastors—in a trial sermon if they were nominated to the pastorate, or in more informal meetings if nominated to other ministries. And they retained a right of veto over these nominees before they were actually ordained. But the lay members of congregations had no right to make formal nominations, no right to participate in the procedures of screening and examination, and no right to initiate dismissal proceedings against a man who had already been ordained. It was these rights which Morely wanted to give to them.

Altogether, then, Morely wanted to vest much more authority, both over church discipline and over the selection of church officers, in the local congregation. And within each local congregation, he wanted to vest much

180

more power in the body of laymen, much less in the company of clergy. In short, he wanted to introduce "democracy" into the government of the church. In fact he used that key word himself. Twice within this book he noted that the form of church government which he was proposing could be labelled "democratic." This is an extremely revealing label, upon which I shall shortly dwell further. But first let me say something about the reception of Morely's ideas.

For these ideas would hardly be very significant if they were only the ideas of a single rather obscure layman, expressed in a single rather rare book. These ideas became, however, the platform of an entire party within the French Reformed Church. And for a decade that party threatened to take over or disrupt the entire structure of that church.

Most of the men attracted to Morely's ideas lived in or near Paris. Recall that this was the area in which his family home was located; to it he naturally returned, about 1564, after having failed to interest Calvinist leaders either in Geneva or Lyon in his reform program. The Paris area also provided Morely with certain natural advantages in seeking support. His family may have had connections with the royal court in earlier generations, and its social standing no doubt secured for him entree he could not find elsewhere. Paris, of course, was a fine place to seek support. For then, as now, it was the unquestioned political and intellectual capital of France. And in this decade Protestantism had much more widespread support in the area than it was to enjoy in succeeding decades.

Among the elements of the Parisian community which Morely came to know, by far the most powerful were clustered around the courts of the high aristocrats who provided political, military, and some administrative leadership to the Huguenot cause. Of these high aristocrats, the one who seems to have become most interested personally in Morely was Odet de Coligny, Cardinal de Châtillon, brother to the even more powerful and better-known

181

Gaspard de Coligny, Admiral of France. Odet de Coligny had become a prince of the Roman Catholic Church solely because of his aristocratic birth and the great political and diplomatic services he could render to the French crown. When his brothers turned Protestant, he did too (apparently not seeing anything particularly incongruous in permitting himself still to be called Cardinal, or in letting his wife by styled "Madame la Cardinale"). Odet had long been a generous patron of intellectuals, and he continued to be one after his conversion. Perhaps it was this interest which drew him to Morely. At any rate it is clear that he personally defended the man in several of the controversies in which Morely became engaged.

It may well be that it was Odet who gave Morely entree to the other important Protestant courts then resident near Paris. Odet's brother the Admiral soon came to know Morely, and was initially impressed by him. Even more important, Morely was introduced to the court of Navarre and secured the position of tutor to the young prince, who, though still a boy, was of the blood royal and titular head of the entire Protestant movement in France. Morely seems, furthermore, to have proved unusually successful as a tutor. Jeanne d'Albret, the Queen of Navarre, later reported that he had taught her son more in three or four months than the boy had learned in the previous seven years.

Attached to these aristocratic courts, or lodged in communities that their power protected, were a number of Calvinist ministers, many of whom had been trained in Geneva. It was inevitable that Morely should also become acquainted with many of them. Among those who apparently did express some interest in his ideas were the chaplains to the Cardinal de Châtillon, the Admiral, and the Prince de Condé, still the chief military commander of the Protestant forces, and second only to young Navarre in social position and legal claim on the throne. One suspects these chaplains of being a little too sensitive to the whims of their masters, however, for as soon as Morely came under attack and lost aristocratic support, they disappeared from his side.

Of the number of ministers who did not leave his side, however, were several of greater quality and importance than any of the chaplains. Perhaps the most interesting was Hugues Sureau, dit du Rosier, who had been a Catholic canon and then a Protestant printer's assistant, who had had some Genevan training, and who in this very decade was proving himself to be one of the most effective Protestant controversialists. In several of the open debates between confessions, sponsored by secular authorities during this period, Sureau represented the Protestant side, and represented it effectively. And to do so he had to be a man of some quality, for this was the period when powerful new Catholic controversialists, some of them Jesuit, were introducing powerful new methods of argument, some of them drawn from the Skeptic philosophy of antiquity, into the continuing debate with Protestants. Sureau was later to make even more of a name for himself by a spectacular double apostasy. He was dramatically converted to Catholicism during the days following the St. Bartholomew's Massacre. And he abandoned his new faith and returned to Calvinist Protestantism with equal éclat, several months later, while on a royally sponsored conversion tour, with an outstanding Jesuit preacher.

Further support came to Morely and his program from certain lay intellectuals who were active in the Protestant movement during these years. Of these the most prominent was Peter Ramus, the royal professor in Paris whose dramatic attacks on Aristotle and other revered authorities of antiquity and whose persuasive proposal of a new system of logic enchanted an entire generation of students and enraged an entire generation of his colleagues. Ramus had been a Protestant sympathizer since about 1561, and he was to die a somewhat inadvertent Protestant martyr during the St. Bartholomew's Massacre. But it was only

183

during the last four years of his life that he was active in Protestant church affairs. During this time he made a tour of a number of Protestant universities in Germany and Switzerland, and then returned to Paris to throw himself with vigor into the activities of the Protestant colloquies and synods of his home province, at the side of Sureau and others, on behalf of the Morely program.

These were not the only men who supported Morely, but they were certainly the most prominent. And their prominence was so great that they could not be dismissed as of no consequence. The clerical leaders of the Calvinist movement had to consider Morely's ideas. And once they had found them unacceptable, they had to campaign against them, in a vigorous and continuing way. Only such a campaign could stem their spread. Moreover Calvin himself, a genius in polemical campaigns as in so many other domains, could no longer direct their activities. He had died, just as Morely began to win powerful support. The challenge posed by Morely, however, was soon met by two of Calvin's most devoted disciples. They were Antoine de la Roche-Chandieu and Theodore Beza.

Chandieu was of a noble family, reasonably well off. He had received a fine education, and was extremely loyal to Calvin. He became a minister of the pivotal Reformed Church in Paris, and had been partly responsible for the conversion to Calvinism of several of the great aristocrats who were so important to the movement. Chandieu had also been something of a political activist. He had embarrassed Calvin and the Reformed Church generally by getting involved in the Conspiracy of Amboise, the harebrained attempt to kidnap the king and kill his regents in 1560. But he was nothing if not orthodox in his theology. And he became ever more willing to follow in ecclesiastical matters the lead of Calvin and the Geneva Company of Pastors. Above all, he was strongly committed to the synodical system. Several times he presided over provincial synods in the Paris area, and he was once chosen Moderator of the French National Synod. At one of the many meetings of these synods which debated the Morely program, Chandieu was charged with preparing a formal reply to Morely. He did so, casting it in the form of a point-by-point refutation of Morely's book. It was duly run through the presses of good Calvinist printers in Geneva and La Rochelle, and widely distributed.

Theodore Beza was the man who more than any other assumed Calvin's place in the entire Reformed movement. He, too, was of a petty French noble family, but he, far more than Morely, even more than Chandieu, was the beneficiary of a fine education. In fact, he was one of the most brilliant products of the great French educational system at the height to which it was goaded by the Renaissance. He was a superb Latinist, a fine Greek scholar, a poet of considerable stature, a skillful logician, and a systematic theologian of real eminence. And Beza was also a man of great practical abilities. These had led to his appointment as first Rector of the University of Geneva, as Moderator of the Geneva Company of Pastors for decades following Calvin's death, and as Moderator of the French National Synod during its particularly important 1571 session in La Rochelle. Beza had also carried out a number of delicate diplomatic missions in support of the Calvinist cause in Germany, in German Switzerland, and in many parts of France. He was constantly being consulted about theological and ecclesiastical problems by church leaders and princes all over Europe. In answer to their queries, he wrote hundreds of shrewd and penetrating letters, which have survived to become one of the finest records of the history of Calvinism during its second generation. It is in these letters, several of which were published by Beza himself, shortly after this controversy died down, that we find the best expressions of his reactions to the movement launched by Morely.

Beza's and Chandieu's reactions were basically defensive. They were designed to defend the authority of the ordained Calvinist clergy and of the regularly convoked synods. Eloquent and vigorous, this defense was based largely on an extended and erudite exegesis of the Bible. It is not my purpose here, however, to describe it in detail, but to focus on one of the many arguments between Morely and Beza and Chandieu. For this particular argument focuses on one subject: Calvinism and Democracy. That last word, "Democracy," indeed, lies at the very heart of the argument I now want to analyze. And "Democracy," in the context which we are now investigating, is a word of many implications. The first of these implications to which I want to draw your attention is of a method of argument. This is the method of argument from analogy. The word "democracy," after all, was invented by the ancient Greeks for the analysis of civil government. To apply it to ecclesiastical government is to assert the existence of a great analogy between the government of the state and the government of the church. And from this great analogy a number of interesting arguments can be developed, which cut in a number of interesting different ways. Not all the men involved in this particular controversy would even accept this analogy. Chandieu, for example, explicitly singled it out for condemnation. But Morely embraced it wholeheartedly, and made deductions from it an integral part of his entire argument. And Beza also accepted it, in order to fight Morely with his own brand of fire.

Morely openly reveals his acceptance of a basic analogy between civil government and ecclesiastical government at the very beginning of his book, which was meant to be the first of a two-volume set: one dealing with the form of ecclesiastical government Morely believed to be enjoined by Scripture and the experience of the church; and a successor, apparently never written, dealing with the form of civil government that Scripture and experience dictated. The basic argument of the first book was, as we have observed, that the form of government God wants for his church is democratic.

Morely's actual use of the word "democratic," however, leads us to a second important implication of that key term. In the sixteenth century, it was almost always a term of condemnation. In those days, to call a government 'democratic' was to damn it. There are solid historical reasons for this reaction. Centuries of political thought in the Christian West on the possible varieties of government, almost always concluding that a well-ordered monarchy was clearly the variety favored if not actually required by God and by Nature, had conditioned most thinking men to instinctive rejection of any form of government in which the people have much share. And this instinctive rejection could only have been fortified by the Renaissance recovery and intensive study of the classical Greek and Roman analyses of the possible forms of government and the relative advantages of each. Both traditions combined to give the very word "democracy" a distinctly negative meaning, to conjure up visions of rule by completely unprincipled and undisciplined mobs subject to no direction but that of occasional vicious and self-serving demagogues.

All of this Morely realized. He was particularly aware of the classical analyses of forms of government, above all of Aristotle's, and he saw that once the analogy between civil and ecclesiastical government was admitted, the classical arguments against democracy could be brought to bear against his proposal. At two points in his book, he grapples directly with this problem. The first time he raises it, he denies that the government he proposes is really a "democracy" in the ancient sense. The two great disadvantages of a democracy in the ancients' eyes, he says, are that it possesses no body of law and no mechanism of administration. However, he argues, both these essential prerequisites can be found in the form of church government he is

187

supporting. Holy Scripture provides the necessary body of law. Through it God has already done the legislative work necessary to the church of defining doctrine and morals. And in it he clearly provides for the selection of a "Moderating Council . . . composed of Pastors and Elders legitimately elected," which becomes the necessary mechanism of administration.

The second time Morely raises the problem of democracy in church government, he goes even further and leans even more heavily on the principle of analogy. He argues that a "democracy" dominated by law is actually the *best* form of civil government. He points to the Athenian and Roman republics as examples of such a government, and insists that they in fact provide the models from which all that is good in contemporary civil government derives. And he bolsters this claim by noting that Aristotle observed that just as a banquet to which many bring dishes is better than one prepared by a single person, so a government taking the advice of many is better than a government controlled by few. The conclusion Morely draws from this line of reasoning, of course, is that the natural reasoning embodied in the authors of antiquity reinforces at this point the scriptural revelation that God wants church government to be democratic. It was not then to his purpose to develop further the notion that democracy was the best form of civil government. Whether he would in fact have developed that notion in his second volume, we shall probably never know. It would have been unusually audacious of him to have done so. And it would almost certainly have cost him the favor of the powerful Huguenot aristocrats who did for a time help him.

Since Morely would have been so vulnerable on this point, it is somewhat surprising that this part of his argument did not draw more fire and draw it earlier. That it did not may be a demonstration that it seemed somewhat peripheral to the fundamental issues at stake in the minds of most of the antagonists involved. But it may be due to a tactical decision that was made by his principal early opponent Chandieu. Chandieu based his refutation almost entirely upon an extended exegesis of the biblical passages which Morely had used. He denied flatly that there could be any analogy between civil and ecclesiastical government, and therefore rejected any argument about the form of ecclesiastical government drawn from secular authorities or natural reason. He charged, indeed, that argument from analogy was a fundamental source of the fallacies of Morely's entire program. Since he based so much of his attack upon this charge, he could hardly scold Morely for introducing democracy into the church and tax him with the classical arguments against that form of government. And so he avoided the subject altogether, and paid no attention to Morely's statements about democracy.

When Beza turned to his public attack on Morely, however, he did not have to worry about such logical scruples. Chandieu had prepared his reasoned and complete refutation of Morely's entire program, to win back the man's supporters or any Protestants disposed to waver in France. Beza wrote his letters largely to counter the influence of Ramus abroad, in intellectual centers where the details of the controversy and Morely himself were hardly known. Beza was thoroughly Aristotelian in many aspects of his own thought, and fully aware of the classic use of the term "democracy." He could furthermore be quite sure that most of his correspondents, and the wider public for whom he published many of these letters, would share this background and this attitude. He therefore seized upon the charge of "democracy" as a useful polemical point to score against Morely and his party, and employed it again and again.

In the most extended of his letters on the subject, addressed to Henry Bullinger, leader of the Reformed Church in Zurich and the most influential contemporary Protestant leader of the Zwinglian tradition, Beza charged that Morely had called the French Reformed Church government an "oligarchy" or "tyranny" and that he was trying to replace it with "the most troublesome and most seditious democracy." This particular attack had its desired effect. Bullinger replied that he had not heard of Morely before, but suspected he must belong to the dreadful sect of Anabaptists, a condemnation that, for Bullinger, may well have been the harshest possible. He could not really believe, however, that Ramus could have held such terrible opinions.

In other letters Beza went further in developing this line of argument. In one he began by denying that the church should be "democratic" and argued that it should rather be a "monarchy," with Jesus Christ as king. He then briefly discussed the role of different orders of clergy, the possibility of "tyranny" arising with an ecclesiastical organization, and relations between clerical and civil authorities. And he returned to the problem of "democracy" by examining and refuting a number of arguments drawn from Scripture by the proponents of more democratic church government.

Throughout these letters, Beza constantly used the classic terms for types of government in discussing his ideal of suitable church government, though not altogether consistently. Sometimes his ideal was a "monarchy" governed by Christ; at other times it was dominated by the "aristocratic" principle, embodied in the consistory. But it was never a "democracy." That term, indeed, was almost invariably coupled with a negatively weighted adjective or two, and Beza was obviously using it as a polemical weapon.

These are the most considered and extended references to "democracy" resulting from this entire controversy. They are very nearly the most complete and the earliest (of which I have knowledge) in the entire sixteenth century. They make it clear that there were thinkers in the earlier stages of the Protestant Reformation who were quite willing to consider analogies between civil and ecclesiastical government and to apply to one sphere arguments

190

drawn from thought about the best form of government in the other sphere.

The debates on church government that I have been discussing came to an abrupt conclusion in 1572. The St. Bartholomew's Massacres, one of the greatest atrocities in all history, not only dealt a crippling blow to Calvinism in France but also wiped out the entire Morely faction, simply because they were most savage in the very areas where he had gained greatest support. Similar debates were to develop in Great Britain, however. They became particularly bitter in the early stages of the great Puritan Revolution, in the 1640s. They led, ultimately, to the creation of the separate Presbyterian and Congregational churches, which remain separate down to this day in most English-speaking countries. I suspect that there were also similar debates in the Netherlands, although I have not as yet investigated this possibility with care. But I have noticed that certain early Dutch synodical acts have phrases in them which are more "democratic" than the parallel phrases in French synodical acts. They sound more like Morely than Beza. And there are other countries in which these debates may have had reverberations.

Some reverberations, indeed, are still with us. The problem of the precise form of government that God wants for his church is again being debated vigorously in all those circles seeking denominational mergers and greater ecumenism. Even the great analogy between government of church and government of state has returned to upset us. It seems to me that this was fundamental to the religious "problem" that figured so prominently in the American presidential election of 1960. In our own times, however, there has been an ironic switch of sides on this issue. In the sixteenth century, Catholics generally insisted that the injection of democracy into the church would lead inevitably to democracy in the state, to the consequent ruin of both. They lashed out against radical groups that were, in fact, democratic. And they even blasted more orthodox

191

groups, like the principal Calvinist churches, for taking steps towards a "democratic" or, as they sometimes put it, a "Swiss" government. In reply, orthodox Calvinists like Chandieu argued that church and state are entirely separate institutions guided by entirely separate principles.

Today many Protestants fear that a totalitarian church can lead to a totalitarian state—and hence question the qualifications of Catholic candidates for public office—while most American Catholics adopt the old Calvinist argument that church and state are radically different.

Which sixteenth-century position should those anxious to maintain the purity of the Calvinist tradition adopt? This question I leave unanswered. Let me only point out that there are three alternatives within that tradition. One can agree with Morely, that God wants democracy in both church and state. One can agree with Beza (and the Catholics), that God opposes democracy in both church and state. Or one can agree with Chandieu, that the two domains should remain entirely separate, and in so doing apply to this problem an old and exceedingly wise piece of advice: "Render unto Caesar the things which are Caesar's; and unto God the things that are God's" (Matthew 22:21).

XI

ERASMUS AND THE REFORMATION

CLARENCE K. POTT

"How much the world, how much the moral and religious culture of Europe owes to Erasmus is not to be calculated. If his name were removed there would be left in the history of our culture a gap not possible to estimate."

This judgment, almost a hundred years old, would meet little disagreement today. It is much more difficult to state clearly the dimensions and nature of the vacuum that would result if the legendary Erasmus of Rotterdam were removed from Western history. To ask it positively, what place *did* he occupy in his age, what chapter in the record

Clarence K. Pott received the doctorate of philosophy from the University of Michigan in 1943. Since that year he has been professor of German there, and in 1960 was appointed chairman of the German Department. He is a member of the American Association of Teachers of German, the Modern Language Association, and the Renaissance Society of America.

of the Western heritage would be left unwritten if he had not lived? To this there is again no single answer: the classicist points to his immense contributions to the revival of classical letters and culture, which we usually summarize under the word "humanism"; the theologian would speak appreciatively of his commentaries on the Bible or of his loving treatment of the church fathers; others regard as paramount his inauguration of new methods and goals for the education of his day; historians of culture, though not in unanimous agreement, are fascinated by his position on the half-political, half-ecclesiastical struggles of his day or his gigantic efforts that resulted in Rome's displacing Paris as the center of higher European culture.

These are the distinctions of scholars. They are important because they are the final summations of the detailed achievements of Erasmus, which, in their effect, changed the cultural development of the Europe of the last four hundred years.

Erasmus would have felt gratified and honored by all these latter-day encomiums. Yet all these endeavors, notable as they are—and to us moderns any one of them may constitute his greatest claim to respectful remembrance—all these endeavors were regarded by Erasmus himself as contributing to his great self-chosen task and hope: a renaissance of Christian faith and practice springing from a return to the sources of the Christian tradition.

Erasmus became for the Northern Europe of the sixteenth century what Petrarca had been for Southern Europe one hundred fifty years before: the herald of a rejuvenation. If the yearning for freedom we hear so often and so plaintively during Erasmus' youth requires an explanation, it surely is to be found in the fact that already very early he had a feeling of destiny, a premonition that *he* was to prepare the way for this cure and for this he needed freedom. In old age he put into words, retrospectively, what had been his youthful goal all the time, and he could claim to have kept his eye fixed on that goal. In 1527, in his sixties, he wrote to a contemporary:

> In all my books you will see me pursue one goal. I raise my voice loudly against the wars which day after day, year after year, are turning almost all of the Christian world upside down. I rebuke the wrongheaded opinions of men everywhere. I am awakening to a purer Christianity, a world which is lying buried in half Jewish ceremonies. To the limit of my ability I am advancing the study of the reviving ancient languages. It is my striving to elicit from even pagan literature a Christian tone.

In his own lifetime, which fell within one of the most violent periods of European history, this Erasmian hope and vision was not at all clear to his contemporaries. The age demanded of its leaders a clear Yea or Nay, acceptance or rejection, an age which demanded passion, not reasonableness. But it was Erasmus' misfortune (or was it wisdom?) that he could see only gray in a world which insisted on black or white. So his life ended, revered still by many who, weary of cruel strife, still dared to avow their affection and respect for him publicly, but detested, for example, by the demonic Luther and viewed with suspicion and fear by many, though not all, the princes of the church to which he remained more faithful than most. History, I suppose, has sided with Luther. *He* had the aim, the weapon, the titanic energy, and the propitious time to achieve a mass following. What Erasmus offered was untimely; its appeal was lost to the masses in the violent storms of the sixteenth century.

Humaneness and reasonableness are virtues which, so it seems, can be admired only in retrospect. Our own age of anxiety, having seen and tasted the fruits of uncontrolled passion, is better able to draw up a fixed reckoning. And thus it was that about twenty years ago another Dutch writer in exile, Hendrik van Loon, invoked the spirit of his countryman Erasmus. From the horror and insanity of World War II Van Loon directed a despairing "Open Letter

195

to Erasmus"—really to the world of course. It was an appeal not to Erasmus the classicist, nor to the linguist, nor even to the explicator of his beloved church fathers. Rather, and all inclusively, the letter was directed to Erasmus as the defender of the Western Christian cultural tradition, a tradition in mortal peril in our own century.

We may designate this as the *essential* Erasmus and it is this Erasmus who engages our attention, but more particularly, an *aspect* of Erasmus which we might name *his ambivalent attitude toward the role of reason as an instrument with which to apprehend reality or truth.* I have called this Erasmian quality the skeptical attitude, and if this characterization is to be justified, we must finally be sure of just what it was that Erasmus was skeptical of.

*   *   *

He was born in Rotterdam, most probably in the year 1466, the illegitimate son of the daughter of a physician (most probably also the town barber) and a village priest, whose name we meet variously as Gerard or Roger. Erasmus himself appears in papal letters as Erasmus Rogerii. Very little is known of his early years. Erasmus' own account in his old age, acutely sensitive as he always remained to the taint of his illegitimate birth, is a rather pathetic attempt to preserve the respectability of his father. But the account cannot be accepted as fact: one of Erasmus' finest biographers, Johan Huizinga, summarizes laconically: "[Erasmus'] sense of chronology was always remarkably ill developed." Or was there a large admixture of deliberate suppresssion?

It is really a pity that we know so little of these parents because they seem to have been people of considerable cultural awareness. The sons (there was a brother) were sent to Deventer to study in the famous school of the chapter of St. Lebuin, an institution that had grown out of that remarkable movement begun toward the end of the fourteenth century, at first confined to the Lowlands and later spreading west, east, and south, which we know today as the *Devotio Moderna*.

It would take us too far afield to engage in a long discussion of the aims and activities of this movement. Let it suffice to say that out of it came, among hundreds of teachers, devout priests, and lay workers of both sexes, such illustrious names as Thomas à Kempis, Rudolph Agricola, and Erasmus himself.

Characteristically Erasmus in later life was coolly objective in his appraisal of this major educative influence of his life: while praising the simplicity and devoutness of the brethren, their social concern, their indignation with the indolence, ignorance, and dissoluteness of the clergy, but especially their thorough cultivation of the study of the ancient classics and languages, he was critical of the narrowness of their intellectual concerns. Neither Wessel Gansvoort, Geert Groote—both founders of the movement—nor even Thomas à Kempis, he felt, had as their ideal the free-spirited forming of the youth in their charge in the many schools which they founded, but this was the plan so ardently championed and demanded by Erasmus. It is tempting but unhistorical to exaggerate the influence these men and their institutes had on the character of the young. They seem to have had surprisingly modern difficulties with the housing and behavior of their charges. We have from the pen of the excellent rector of the school at Alkmaar, Johannes Murmellius, an inaugural address of 1514 in which he found it necessary to issue the following regulations for his charges:

1. Students are to conduct themselves courteously and decorously with their roommates and with the burghers in whose homes they reside.
2. They are not to insult anyone, nor to appropriate anything which does not belong to them.
3. They are to sleep in their rooms and to refrain from walking the streets at night.
4. Visiting of wine houses is forbidden; nor are they to frequent

197

> pastry shops; much less are they to associate with "frivolous" women.
> 5. They are forbidden to carry swords or daggers.
> 6. They are to be soberly dressed and their hair is to be clipped short.
> 7. Sundays and holidays students are required to attend mass; during the week they must be punctual in their class attendance, be attentive to their teachers, to recite at home what they have heard, and to prepare the lessons for the following day.
> 8. Their motto is to be: to live well and to speak Latin.

Such was the educational ideal when Erasmus was a boy, and to its improvement and cultivation he devoted much of his life effort.

The death of the parents while Erasmus and his brother were still young brought about a decision by the three guardians about which there has been considerable dispute. Huizinga is probably correct in surmising that the choice of the monastic life—by the guardians, not the two young men—was dictated to be sure by a desire to please God but it happened also to be a way for them to rid themselves of a troublesome responsibility. At any rate Erasmus entered the monastery of Steyn, near Gouda, and in 1488 he took his vows.

Erasmus' account of his life at Steyn, written in later life, cannot be taken at face value. The evidence, mainly letters, shows little of the thorough aversion to monastic life which he later claimed to have felt. He even wrote a "Praise of Monastic Life" and tries to explain this by stating that he wrote this piece "to please a friend who wished to decoy a cousin." This is most probably a bit of fable. The life at Steyn was by no means completely tasteless and sterile. He found companions there; he had at least some freedom to continue the studies begun as a youth; there were even among his superiors those who encouraged precocious young men and who were able to provide intellectual stimulation.

What then are we to make of this curious contradiction?

Some of his unfriendly critics, then and since, have ascribed it to a basic duplicity in his character and condemn him as a man ultimately incapable of making moral decisions. This easy conclusion, it seems to me, is not only inconsistent with our total reading of Erasmus, it is superficial and fails to grasp the significance of the extraordinary psychological complexity of the man's nature.

Erasmus' account of his own reaction to the monastic life at Steyn exhibits for the first time a peculiar quality of his mind, a conscious but very subtle recognition that even so-called simple facts and truths are never simple and univocal, but always complex and equivocal. In the present instance it is quite possible, even necessary I think, to look upon Erasmus' reaction to the monastic life at Steyn as being thus complex; that a part of his being, the empirical, pragmatic side of his nature, made the most of those opportunities at Steyn that satisfied his love of philological study. This and the friendships he found there he could enjoy. But there was an unengaged side of his nature, a private Erasmus that he guarded jealously and all his life from prying eyes, a side that he never consciously revealed. It is a condition akin to the loneliness of the artist or of the saint. And this found no contact in Steyn; it never found contacts; such natures never do and they are always misjudged. Few men in the history of culture have suffered more from this kind of misjudgment than Erasmus.

There is one point of criticism by Erasmus of the type of education and educational theory which prevailed at Steyn which we ought to note: he speaks of the ultra-puritanical object of this education, and then of the rigid discipline "intent on breaking the personality." This is revelatory and expresses his fear of having the sanctity of his being invaded by a regimen which fails to respect the sovereignty of personality. How modern this is!

These are the beginnings of Erasmus, and during these early years all the many sides of this complex personality are already evident. It has been remarked that "it is one of the peculiarities of Erasmus' mental growth that it records no violent crises." This is true, and it is another way of saying that the permanent "set" of his mind had come early. All experiences and writings subsequent to his youth are merely extensions and variations of his way of looking at life and man—no sudden dramatic illuminations, as for example in Martin Luther, and therefore also no tempestuous, demonic driving to mold the opinions of his fellow man.

For us, as indeed during Erasmus' own lifetime, the historically most important complex of events grew out of his collision with the Reformation unleashed by Luther, or rather the encounter with Luther himself. This is a distinction of some consequence. For it is an historical fact that Luther's criticisms of the church, its ceremonials, the excesses of many of the clergy—all these had been uttered constantly by Erasmus (and indeed by others) with all the virtuosity of style and sardonic sharpness of pen of which the great Latin master was capable.

The facts of this clash are pretty well known; the judgments based on these facts are not at all unanimous. A later age has come to understand that here was much more than two sets of opposing intellectual formulations. History and its conditionings, the temperament of the protagonists, the psychological predispositions of the personalities involved—all these had as much to do with the dispute (and with our own final judgments) as had the theological issues of the case. It is possible, though not completely satisfying, to set up a number of antinomies which describe but do not exhaust the matter. Luther, the theologian, insisted upon the theological doctrine of justification by faith as the mysterious essence of man's relationship to God; Erasmus, while not disputing the priority of this, was more concerned with the ethical implication of this doctrine for the Christian life—quite in the spirit of Thomas à Kempis' *Imitatio Christi*. Someone has given this a homely formulation: Luther asks "what must I *do* to be saved?" and answers "there is nothing that I *can do*"; Erasmus asks "what must I do now that I am saved?"

This is the heart of the matter, but the complications are legion. And if it is true to say that there are important and fundamental intellectual differences between Luther and Erasmus, it is much more important to note the *temperamental, emotional,* and *personality* differences between these two. Both men quite possibly became victims, each in his own way, of a grandiose one-sidedness, dictated not really by fundamental differences of religious convictions but by differences of historical and personality conditionings. Luther, ever suspicious of Erasmus' passion for pagan learning, was philosophically the disciple of William of Occam, the man of absolute distinctions; Erasmus of the contemplative, scholarly, and almost pietistic St. Jerome. Luther could finally dismiss the enigmatic Netherlander with the harsh absolute: "The human stands higher with him than the divine." Erasmus in an equally extreme moment ejaculated: "Saint Socrates, pray for me." Between such positions no bridge could be formed.

*   *   *

Until fairly recently the opinions of scholars and historians of religion fell roughly into these two camps. In the introduction to a recent translation of Erasmus' *Enchiridion Militis Christiani,* Professor Himelick sums up with admirable precision the real difference between the two men and the two positions:

> The "tragic defect" of Erasmus, according to Huizinga, was his inability, or unwillingness to draw "ultimate conclusions." One wonders, though, as Erasmus must have wondered, if the world has not had a plethora of "ultimate conclusions" which make men willing to kill and die, but never to be reasonable. This *was* his ultimate conclusion, and of course it lacks the compelling intensity of passion that produced a More or a Tyndale, a Servetus or a Savonarola. Like Montaigne, Erasmus would follow no cause into the fire. However, men willing to

201

be burned for causes have frequently been willing to burn others. For an Erasmus, the only valid goal of the Christian faith was one which reciprocal martyrdoms would not reach: a world in which men "wish for good, pray for good, act for good to all men" on the ground that they are all "mutual members of one another."

We could do much worse, it seems, and ordinarily we do.

One important point is worth noting: Whatever absolute sides we choose today, the for and against were not all so clear during Erasmus' own day. There is a moving testimony by an illustrious contemporary of both Luther and Erasmus which we may take as the expression of attitudes current in the early sixteenth century. Albrecht Dürer, certainly not an intellectual or a theologian in the sense of either Erasmus or Luther, but a great artist and devout Christian and good Catholic, visited the Lowlands in 1521. While staying in Antwerp a rumor became current that Martin Luther had been arrested on his return from the Diet of Worms, presumably by the emperor's soldiers and in violation of the free conduct which Luther had been granted; he had probably been murdered. The effect on Dürer was devastating and he broke out in a lament that the voice of this great champion of the true religion was now stilled and Christianity lay prostrate. But then he adds these remarkable words: "O Erasme Roderadame, where are you? Behold what the unjust tyranny of worldly power, the power of darkness has done. Hear, O knight of Christ, ride forth beside the Lord, protect the truth, gain the martyr's crown, after all you are already a little old man. I have heard that you have given yourself another two years in which you can yet do something." I cite this passage only to show that contemporaries (and in the case of Dürer we may assume that this is the voice of many) looked upon Erasmus *then* as a champion of Christianity. The issue was to the mind of sixteenth-century Christian Europe not at all clear. Erasmus had supporters in both camps: Philipp Melanchthon, usually regarded as the heir of Luther, was, for example, both by intellectual interest and temperament closer to Erasmus than to Luther.

The reading public had sufficient opportunity to be informed; both Luther and Erasmus were prolific writers. Where Luther swept readers along with irresistible vigor and eloquence in his numerous polemics, notably his magnificent *Freedom of the Christian*, the ethical emphasis of such a work as Erasmus' *Adagia* (this work consisting of some 800 Latin proverbs with commentaries) was of great effect upon the educated. *The Enchiridion Militis Christiani* likewise generated real excitement among its contemporary readers.

Professor Himelick remarks that, though today's secular society looks upon such works as the *Enchiridion* as mild historical curiosities, "in the Renaissance, however, their heartfelt preoccupation with questions of faith and doctrine did exist, and it helped make the *Enchiridion* a best seller. First published in 1503, it had more than thirty editions within the next twenty years—in French, Dutch, Spanish, German, and English—the accounts of an English bookseller for 1520 show that a third of all sales to his countrymen were of works by Erasmus and that the *Enchiridion* was one of the favorites."

It should be remembered, then, that for considerable time men looked upon the two protagonists as complementary, not hostile, pursuing the same ends but with different methods. No inevitable conflict was felt to exist between the writings of the two men. Erasmus applauded Luther's initial efforts and Luther in turn welcomed the seconding voice of the renowned humanist. By 1520 the rift had appeared, and it came to an irremediable break by 1524. In that year Erasmus had published his *De Libero Arbitrio* (On Free Will) in which he argued, typically, that there was no compulsion on man to yield to his baser nature—again the ethical emphasis. Luther's answer, *De Servo Arbitrio*, developed the thesis that since the fall of man his will too has become so defective that it naturally and perversely inclines toward evil.

The nature of the intellectual climate of the sixteenth century, in which Erasmus lived, seems to me to demand some discussion of the clash with Luther. Erasmus himself avowed as his chief interest the enhancement of faith and morals. Without taking cognizance of this there is simply no point in discussing Erasmus. And yet there is an even wider dimension of the man and, it seems to me, an even more fundamental one, perhaps more meaningful to us.

For it was more than temperament, more than a different psychological predisposition, which makes Erasmus a natural opponent of Luther, which marks a parting of the ways even from his great Christian humanist contemporaries, e.g. his beloved friend Sir Thomas More. It was, I believe, a unique attitude toward the intellect and its constructions which makes him a man apart. The age was by historical necessity positivistic. Luther *knew* and Erasmus felt compelled to ask: what did he know? The original Lutheran insight, Erasmus could agree (and we with him), was illumination—all the rest, Erasmus was convinced, was interpretation, i.e. intellectual construction. And here we are confronted with a paradox: Erasmus, the man of mind, was not at all sure of the reliability of mind, and more important and springing from this skepticism, he was certainly not willing to base *ultimate* decisions on purely intellectual constructions. And such he took much of the Lutheran doctrine to be! Grand constructions to be sure, necessary perhaps, even understandable as evolving from the historical situation of sixteenth-century Christendom, but to attribute universal and final validity to them, to base concrete and irrevocable action upon them—to that Erasmus said No! His *practical*, one might say, his *pragmatic* sense told him that surely one of the tests of the validity of any concept was its test in life. He was not fighting with oratorical weapons, it was not a desire to rout the enemy with words which made him write in 1529, seven years before his death, to a friend of the Reformation:

> Behold these evangelical people, and observe whether they are less devoted to luxury, to self indulgence, to greed than are those whom you condemn! Show me one whom that gospel transformed from a glutton into a man of moderation, from a cruel into a compassionate man, from a robber into a generous man. . . . May I ask how much wiser and better you have become?

In this way Erasmus stated his conviction that any belief without a practical, ethical consequence is meaningless. And at least one time he became very pointed, almost savage, in answering those who accused him of vacillation, even cowardice: "I am willing, if God gives me the strength, to die for Him—but to die for Martin Luther— NO!" It could not be said more plainly than that.

The significance of the strictures Erasmus placed on the intellect goes deeper. Certainly he was, as we have seen, a man who did much for learning, for the encouragement of the life of the mind. But he also feared placing theological subtleties in the hands of the half-educated masses. The whole *Enchiridion* is an exhortation to common folk to cultivate a kind of Christian primitivism that goes back to the scriptural sources rather than the trifling subtleties of argument invented by the professional scholastics.

All this, however, makes of Erasmus a troublesome, unsatisfactory, enigmatic character. He is hard to pin down and, incidentally, he intentionally always keeps a part of himself hidden. *Why is this*? Are the charges of dishonesty and evasiveness true after all? Or is it something deeper? Did he know something of the everlastingly ambivalent nature of intellectual "truth"—that "principles" to which his age and ours constantly pay homage constantly need redefining, that words do not mean the same to all men in all generations? It may be argued that not Erasmus is elusive, *the apprehension of "truth" is*.

Erasmus not only believed this because he experienced

paradox in his own life—he lived it. A pope accepted the dedication of his New Testament, but an emperor who was an ardent supporter of the papacy had the servants of the Inquisition collect the copies and destroy them. Contemporaries and countrymen of his were burned at the stake for the sake of opinions which were his, but he would have denied his opinions rather than bring one of his fellow men to the scaffold. A born Netherlander, he was at the same time a born cosmopolitan. By birth a member of the nameless mass, he hated neither the masses, nor the burghers, nor the nobility. Obedient son of the church, he was tireless in tormenting its leaders. The greatest terror of stupid monks was the former Augustinian, but he did not find that the Lutheran preachers were a gain for Christian culture. Crowned heads honored him with their friendship, but even the wearers of three-cornered hats did not escape his criticism. He was probably the wisest man of his time and is remembered today as the praiser of folly.

*   *   *

Contemporaries viewed *The Praise of Folly* as one of the many popular satires directed at the social and ecclesiastical practices of the age and no more than that. And, indeed, it seems clear that with it Erasmus hoped to strike a heavy blow in a jocular vein.

It is Erasmus' most difficult work. Unlike Sebastian Brant's *Ship of Fools* of 1494, which was a straightforward castigation of a host of social and moral ills, *The Praise of Folly* is the most characteristic of the mind of its author *in that the role of Folly changes.*

His attack on various ecclesiastical orders—this is its first level—is devastating. Folly, in eulogy of herself, proclaims that without her the clerics would be the most wretched people on earth, for without Folly's blinders their absurd self-esteem, their sense of virtue because of their ceremonial observances, would be impossible. How desperate these clerics would be, says Folly, if I did not hide from them what Pharisees they really are.

But now a shift occurs. Folly begins to lose her character as a wicked deluder but remains a sort of inevitable inclination of men. There are some hilarious, but not bitter, passages dealing, for example, with the absurd ceremonials that attend the English passion for the hunt.

Now come the paragraphs where Folly begins almost to assume the status of a virtue; that is, we can no longer condemn her outright if we are not to deprive men of a *useful* quality that adds an innocent and pleasant diversion to life and indeed helps make life more supportable. Gradually this role of Folly takes on prominence, and it seems to me that this is Erasmus himself speaking. Because of his dubious origin and difficult youth, Erasmus could easily have become a misanthrope. In his loneliness he finds solace in the fact that all human actions and motivations have their humorous side. Just as deeply as Holbein, who furnished the illustrations for *The Praise of Folly*, Erasmus felt that human life is like the performance of a Dance of Death. The presence of the god, Terminus—The End—is always evident. But this remembrance is not a source of bitterness: he cannot ponder any subject, no matter how serious, without in his imagination noting that looking over the shoulders of the goddesses, Virtue, Truth, Beauty, there is the ubiquitous smiling face with the cap with bells, Phantasy or Folly. Faith, Knowledge, Love, Enthusiasm, Self-Sacrifice seem to be serious only up to a point and they cannot remain serious without a saving, preserving, grain of Folly. Is not this the role of Cervantes' Sancho Panza and of Shakespeare's Falstaff?

The highest level of paradox is reached when Erasmus finally dares to speak, referring to biblical texts, of the "Folly of the Cross," the "Foolishness of God which is wiser than men," of Christianity itself as a divine comedy, of Christian piety which, despising all earthly advantages to gain a heaven, becomes a kind of holy insanity.

207

It is the final recognition by Erasmus that no matter how great the exertion of man's powers of reason, he will not be able to fathom the mystery of his own being, and that our existence remains finally an impenetrable mixture of the comic and the tragic, sublime and pedestrian. And that I take to be the benevolent Erasmian skepticism of the intellect. Because man is unable to arrive at absolutes *with his intellect*, it behooves him indeed to be reasonable and tolerant.

He was the living healthy intelligence of his age. Born a Netherlander (which he remained), he loved Basel. He did not wish to live in a corner with a book, rather in the mountains with a printing press. He was conscious that with this lever he could move a world; and his finest patent of nobility is perhaps that despite this dangerous feeling of personal power, he always remained so humble and so simple.

XII

ARMINIUS AS A REFORMED THEOLOGIAN

CARL BANGS

Jacobus Arminius (died 1609), a pastor and professor in Holland, was at the center of theological controversy in the Dutch Reformed Church of his time. After his death he became a byword for heresy in Reformed and Lutheran circles. His name became attached to schools of theology as diverse as Dutch Remonstrantism, Anglican high church-manship, Wesleyan revivalism, and New England liberal Puritanism. References to Arminius were made from with-in partisan camps and were marked by the praise or odium,

Carl Bangs was awarded the Ph.D. degree by the University of Chicago in 1958. He has taught at Olivet Nazarene College and St. Paul School of Theology in Kansas City, and in 1966 was a Fulbright Lecturer at the University of Leiden, Netherlands. His articles have appeared in Church History *and* Religious Life; *and he is the author of* German-English Theological Word List, The Communist Encounter, De Herstructurering van de theologische opleiding, *and* Arminius: A Study in the Dutch Reformation.

not to mention ignorance, which stemmed from the particular viewpoint being defended or attacked. The upshot was to reinforce the sense of distance between Arminius and Reformed theology. The sweep of modern movements has to some degree blurred old party lines, and new research has put the Reformation itself in new perspectives. It should be both necessary and possible, then, to reexamine the relationship of Arminius to Reformed theology to the enhancement of our understanding of the Dutch Reformation and of the place of Arminius in it.

Some preliminary observations about the Dutch Reformation are in order. First, it was forged amidst the political confusion of the struggle for independence from Spain. This means that the story is broken, fragmentary, disjointed. The movement of reform was often interrupted or even terminated in local instances by deaths, persecutions, deportations, plagues, harassments, and the changing tides of military campaigns. Furthermore, our knowledge is fragmentary because of the destruction of the archives by war, flood, and accident. Generalizations about the Dutch Reformation are difficult to support. Indeed, it is scarcely one movement in the sense that the English or Saxon or Genevan Reformations were unitary. At the same time, it took form even earlier than the nation itself did. The Dutch Reformed Church can be said to antedate the Dutch nation.

Second, its religious and theological roots are diverse. Broadly speaking, there was an intermingling of indigenous reforming movements and movements imported from Switzerland, France, and the Palatinate, among others. To select only one of these traditions as the norm is gratuitous. In controversies over the authority of the Heidelberg Catechism, for instance, the question was raised as to the propriety of being bound by a non-Dutch formula. There were those who supported stricter Calvinist confessions, or none at all. The consequence is that the Dutch Reformation is *sui generis*, not to be subsumed under categories derived from Swiss or Palatine Reformed Churches or seen as a mere extension of them.

Third, the Dutch Reformation was dominated by no one figure, be he politician, churchman, or theologian. In many local instances it was a lay movement, with the lay magistrates instituting the reform of the church and then inviting ministers from outside to come to preach and administer the sacraments and other ministerial functions. A prime example is Amsterdam. The first overt steps toward a magisterial Reformation were taken in 1566. The leaders were merchants. Catechetical instruction and preaching were provided by Pieter Gabriel and Jan Arendsz. The former was an Amsterdam resident, no formally ordained minister, and the second, a basketmaker, was an itinerant reforming preacher invited to Amsterdam by one of the laymen, Reynier Cant. A third preacher, Nicholas Scheltius, was likewise imported by the laymen. The movement was abortive and the Protestant leaders were exiled, but when Amsterdam was finally Protestantized at the Alteration of 1578, the pattern was repeated. For the first Reformed service, held on May 11, 1578, it was necessary to bring in a minister from Delft, but the Reformed regime had already been established by the laymen themselves. Elders and deacons were chosen on May 24, but it was not until August that two permanent ministers were chosen and installed. One, Johannes Cuchlinus, was from Hesse. The other, Petrus Hardenberg, about whom little is known, came to Amsterdam from Emden. The imported clergy usually brought with them a theology more precise in its Calvinism than that of the lay church leaders. The best-known merchant theologian was Laurens Jacobsz Reael, whose catechism was marked by an irenic and broad spirit.[1]

It is customary among some historians to find the true character of the Dutch Reformation in the decisions of the several synods which occurred in the late sixteenth and early seventeenth centuries. The synods reveal a great deal, but they cannot be accepted as adequate indexes to the "true" Reformed Church any more now than in their own time. In their own time they were less universal in character and less than compelling in authority. Professor G. J. Hoenderdaal points out that synods previous to the Synod of Dort (1618-19) had lacked full status as national synods, as that status was understood at the time.[2] The earlier Synod of Dort (1574) had not been called by the States General. The Synod of The Hague (1586) was so dominated by the Earl of Leicester, who supported one-sidedly a high Calvinist position with respect to church order, that after his forced resignation in 1588 it was discredited in the eyes of the states and its strictures on the role of the magistrate in the call of the pastor were widely ignored. The earlier synods of Wesel (1568) and Emden (1571), held outside the country, had also failed to meet the criteria, which were essentially (1) authority from the States General and (2) universal representation.

It was only the Synod of Dort of 1618-19 which could claim effectively the status of a national synod. This has led historians to fall into an anachronism, that is, to judge affairs prior to Dort by decisions first made at Dort. Dort, whatever its merits or faults, did accept from among the many strands of Dutch Reformed tradition only certain positions with respect to both doctrine and church order. In the attempt to determine the position of any particular person, movement, or doctrine in the Dutch Reformed Church prior to Dort, it is necessary to avoid the anachronism of imposing the judgments of Dort to periods prior to their enactment.

This reminds us that there was one broad stream of Dutch Reformed life and thought which was declared out of bounds by Dort. At the time it was called Remonstrantism or Arminianism, but it antedated both the Remonstrance of 1610 and Arminius. It is sometimes called the "Dutch National Reformation." L. Knappert, in a chapter on "De nationaal gereformeerden," mentions Angelus Merula, priest at Heenvliet; Anastasius Veluanus (Jan Gerritsz Verstege), priest at Garderen; Stephanus Sybrandi Sylvius, priest at Tjum; Henricus Geldorpius of Groningen; and Petrus Bloccius, who appears as a preceptor at the Latin School in Leiden in 1559.[3] Other writers include earlier figures—Cornelis Hoen, Willem Gnapheus, Hinne Rode, and Jan de Bakker (Joannes Pistorius). Hubert Duifhuis, reforming priest or conservative reformer in Utrecht, should be added to the list, and the group would include Cornelis Kooltuin, priest in Delft, and such names as Gerard Blokhoven, Tako Sybrants, and Caspar Coolhaes. They did not constitute a unified movement. Many of them hoped at first for reform within the Roman Church. Merula continued to wear his priest's robes while he reformed the Mass. Erasmus was influential among them. Bloccius spoke for many of them when he declared his independence of Menno, Luther, and Calvin. We must know only Christ, he said. The church does not save us; only Jesus and his teaching. Such men were spiritual heirs of the Sacramentists who did not take up with Anabaptism. But neither did they take up with Calvin. Veluanus was explicit about that. On predestination he said, "Here we must hold with the primitive Christians that God has eternally decreed within himself to help and save by his Holy Spirit such persons who use all possible means to be instructed, and continue obedient when they are called, and in like manner to strengthen and confirm others in the way of salvation who earnestly beg it of him." The fact that this more diffuse source of the Dutch Reformation could embrace the humanist or "Libertine" Dirk Volckertsz Coornhert, who belonged to no church, should not shut our eyes to the inclusion also of Johannes à Lasco, Joannes Utenhove, and Martinus Micronius, who can scarcely be described as Calvinists. Nor should the movement be described as a "third force," something not genuinely related to what emerged as the Dutch Reformed Church. There was an intermingling of the "Dutch National Reformation" and more strictly Calvinist-Reformed currents, and they did not get segregated until Dort.[4]

Conflict there was, of course, between the National Reformers and the stricter Calvinists. It turned first on the question of church order, particularly the role of the magistrate in the government of the church. A notable outbreak of this controversy occurred in Leiden between the magistrates and C. Coolhaes, representing the "National Reformation," and Pieter Cornelisz, Coolhaes' colleague in the Leiden ministry, who represented the stricter Calvinists, among whom were the numerous refugees from the southern provinces. Lambertus Danaeus, arriving in 1581 as the new Professor of Theology, jumped into the fray on the side of the Calvinists.[5] Only later would it become a controversy over the doctrines of grace: predestination was not the issue in the Leiden affair. The result would be a growing polarity, or perhaps more accurately a growing recognition of the polarity, between two broad parties within the Dutch Reformed Church. Gerard Brandt, the seventeenth-century Remonstrant historian, was to observe that in this period the word "Reformed" came to have two meanings, one for the older Hollanders and another for the newly arrived refugee Calvinist clergy. In 1597 the Amsterdam burgomaster C. P. Hooft complained that the consistory was coming under the domination of outsiders who did not understand the nature of Holland, where steadiness and peace abounded, but introduced alien quarrels.

It is in this context that the question about Arminius is to be approached. Can he be regarded properly as a Dutch Reformed theologian? A number of points can be offered to support the affirmative.

First, he was a native Hollander, born in the ancient Dutch town of Oudewater, educated in the Latin School at Utrecht, and the twelfth student to enroll in the new national university at Leiden. His point of view was that of the indigenous Dutch Reformers who saw the refugees

from the southern provinces in some respects as inter-
lopers.

Second, he knew no other church identification than
the Dutch Reformed Church. Although his parents could
have been Roman Catholics in the years before his birth,
his own earliest training was Protestant and Reformed.

Third, he became a protege of Amsterdam in 1581, just
three years after its Reformation. Under life contract to
serve the ministry of the Dutch Reformed Church there,
he was Amsterdam's first such fosterling.

Fourth, his advanced theological education was at the
academy at Geneva under Calvin's successor, Theodore
Beza, who expressed his esteem for his Dutch student in a
letter to the authorities in Amsterdam.

Fifth, in 1588 he became the tenth person inducted into
the Dutch Reformed ministry in Amsterdam, and the first
Hollander in that position, the others having been imported from outside the country.

Sixth, in 1603 he became the first Dutch professor of
theology at Leiden, and its first alumnus in that position.
In 1605 his colleagues honored him with the office of
Rector Magnificus. Although opposed by refugee Calvinist
clergy in the consistories and synods, he was sustained in
his post by the curators and burgomasters, laymen all.

Seventh, his thought-world was that of Calvinism. He
was no Roman Catholic, Lutheran, Anabaptist, or "Libertine." He could speak of all these in the third person, and
he defended the Dutch Reformed Church against all of
these and against the English dissenters in Holland. His
doctrinal concerns were those of Calvinism, and at many
points he followed precisely the teaching he had received
in Geneva, for example, the sacraments. Underlying his
writing is the literature of world Calvinism, its confessions
and its theologians.

At this point it is helpful to pause to consider his
relation to Calvin. Arminius' own words, often quoted, can
be taken at face value. When accused of turning his stu-

215

dents to the writings of Coornhert and of the Jesuits, he replied:

> So far from this, after the reading of Scripture, which I strenuously inculcate, and more than any other (as the whole university, indeed, the conscience of my colleagues will testify) I recommend that the *Commentaries* of Calvin be read, whom I extol in higher terms than Helmichius [an Amsterdam minister, a strict Calvinist foe of Arminius] himself, as he owned to me, ever did. For I affirm that in the interpretation of Scriptures Calvin is incomparable, and that his *Commentaries* are more to be valued than anything that is handed down to us in the writings of the Fathers—so much so that I concede to him a certain spirit of prophecy in which he stands distinguished above others, above most, indeed, above all. His *Institutes*, so far as respects Commonplaces, I give out to be read after the Catechism as a more extended explanation. But here I add—with discrimination, as the writings of all men ought to be read.[6]

To speak of Calvinism in this connection raises a problem. The modern approach would be to compare the doctrinal statements of Arminius with those of Calvin. The result would be a mixture of agreement and dissent, with possibly no less agreement or more dissent than would be found in many later Calvinists, especially those of our time. But in Holland in Arminius' time Calvin was not the central point of reference. He had receded into the recent past. In international Calvinism the leading figure was Beza. In Holland, however, the standard against which doctrine was coming to be tested was the Belgic Confession and the Heidelberg Catechism. What did Arminius say about these formularies, and how, in fact, did his theology compare with them?

Arminius, under pressure of attack within the consistory in Amsterdam, found it necessary to affirm his faithfulness to Confession and Catechism as early as 1593. He made such professions repeatedly, as in June 1605, in his response to deputies of the Synods of North and South Holland. In December 1606, under attack this time from

216

the Synod of South Holland, he responded that he was studying the Confession and Catechism and that if he had any criticisms of them he would make them at a proper time and place. When the Preparatory Convention for a National Synod met in May 1607, Arminius was among the delegates who argued that members of the Synod should be bound only by Scripture, not by the Confession and Catechism. The issue was whether or not the Synod would have the freedom to revise the formularies. But the next year, in his letter to the Palatine Ambassador Hippolytus à Collibus, Arminius persisted in defending his orthodoxy. "I confidently declare," he said, "that I have never taught anything, either in the church or in the university, which contravenes the sacred writings that ought to be with us the sole rule of thinking and of speaking, or which is opposed to the Belgic Confession or to the Heidelberg Catechism, that are our stricter formularies of consent."[7] In his "Declaration of Sentiments" to the States of Holland and West Friesland on October 30, 1608, he challenged one and all to show that he had ever propounded any doctrine "in conflict with either the Word of God or the Confession of the Dutch Churches." If his writings should contradict the Confession, he says, he should be liable to just punishment; but how much more should that punishment be were his writings to be found contrary to the word of God![8] It was a subtle reminder that the Bible has authority over the Confession. And in the last, bitter conference at The Hague in August 1609, Arminius still maintained his position. He died in October, steadfast in his profession of loyalty to the Confession (the Heidelberg Catechism did not remain such a central issue at this time and is not mentioned) but also firm in the belief that human formulas must be subject to the word of God and that it is incumbent on the church to examine them anew respecting their faithfulness to that word.

So much for his profession. What about the substance of his theology?

So far as Confession and Catechism were concerned, there were questions on only two or three articles. The most problematic was Article 16 of the Belgic Confession. In its original form, prior to revisions made at Dort, it read as follows:

> We believe that whereas the whole posterity of Adam is fallen into ruin and damnation through the guilt of the first man, God showed himself to be such as he is, namely, merciful and just: merciful in that he delivers and saves out of this ruination those whom he in his eternal and unchangeable council, through his pure goodness has elected [wtuersien] and chosen in Jesus Christ our Lord, without any consideration of their good works; and in that he leaves the others in their fall and ruin wherein they themselves have cast themselves.[9]

Many Reformed theologians of recent years have been willing to relegate this article to the historical dustbin. Not Arminius. He saw in it two possible meanings: one, that those who are "chosen in Jesus Christ" are believers; the other, that God selects certain persons to be believers. He accepted the article under the first interpretation, which he regarded as its natural and unforced import. His opponents held to the second as the only permissible interpretation. The question was moot, for no formal decision had been made concerning it. It is anachronistic to read Arminius out of the Dutch Reformed Church for taking the position he did.

Another point in the Belgic Confession where a problem could arise was Article 14. It states that man "has wilfully submitted himself to sin and thereby to death and the curse." Arminius found no problem here and cited this passage in support of his position in the "Declaration of Sentiments." The intervening Article 15, "Of Original Sin," was no problem to Arminius. The only other point of possible dissent would have been Article 36, on the magistracy. In Arminius' time, that is, prior to revisions made at Dort, it ascribed to the magistrates the oversight of affairs not only political but also ecclesiastical. Arminius, in the tradition of the National Reformers, accepted this. [10]

With the Heidelberg Catechism Arminius found no difficulty at all, no need of discriminating interpretations. Question 20 was entirely to his liking:

> Q. Will all men, then, be saved through Christ as they became lost through Adam?
> A. No. Only those who, by true faith, are incorporated into him and accept all his benefits.

An eighth argument that can be advanced in support of regarding Arminius as a Dutch Reformed theologian is that, in spite of occasional allegations to the contrary, he was not an Anabaptist, a Socinian, a "Libertine," a Pelagian, or a crypto-Roman Catholic. He was well aware of all these positions and of the difficulties they entailed from a Reformed point of view. He rejected the Anabaptist views of sacraments and magistracy, although he did indeed draw back from pursuing them as heretics. On the doctrine of the Trinity he eschewed Socinianism, although he did prefer biblical to metaphysical language. His defense of Origen's refusal to call Christ *autotheos* [possessing in himself the divine nature] was developed into a definite subordinationism only in some of his followers. He affirmed a full Trinitarian dogma in his own writings. He was too deeply involved in Reformed theology to be a "Libertine," and only on certain political issues, and on the question of toleration, did he have a marked affinity with D. V. Coornhert. He knew all about Pelagianism, semi-Pelagianism, and the like, and observed wryly that there might be a better fraction which would come closer to the truth. As for being a Catholic, the charges can be explained only by malice borne along by the tide of hysteria that accompanied the war with Spain. And it can be added that he was no schismatic. Near the end of his life, when it appeared that his enemies might be able to remove him from his professorship, he vowed that he would step aside quietly, remain loyal to the church, and allow no new sect to be formed around him.

Why, then, did he become the focal point of so much controversy?

A large part of the answer lies in the conflicts of his time in both church and state, the story of which occupies a great part of my *Arminius*. At the same time it must be admitted that he attempted one theological device which was justly criticized, namely, the doctrine of the predestination of individuals on the basis of foreseen faith. In his "Declaration of Sentiments" he defined his doctrine of predestination in terms of four decrees. The first was the election or appointment of Jesus Christ to obtain salvation, for Arminius a rejection of supralapsarianism but for us a fascinating anticipation of Pierre Maury and Karl Barth. The second was the election of the church, that is, of those who are in Christ by faith. The third was the appointment of "necessary, sufficient, and powerful [efficacious] means of repentance and faith." The fourth, where he felt it necessary to speak of individual election, was a "decree to save certain particular persons and to damn others" on the basis of God's foreknowledge of future faith and unbelief. It moved on the ground of predestination from the divine will to the divine knowledge of man's will, according to his critics. From a modern perspective, it concedes too much to philosophical determinism and moves too far away from the christological basis of predestination. Arminius did not intend either of these consequences, but his proposal was not as helpful as he thought. At the same time, it was scarcely an innovation in the Dutch Reformed Church. Veluanus had taught the same thing forty years earlier, and there were many others who would have agreed.

There were some points at which he did not teach what the Reformed Churches would teach in later centuries. His doctrines of imputation were not to be adopted by later Reformed thought, by and large, but they had not been condemned in his own time. His exegesis of Romans 7 and Romans 9 did not find wide favor in later Reformed thought. He taught that a believer could not fall from grace, but his suggestion that a believer could cease believing and as a non-believer be lost would be hotly contested in many Reformed circles. His "Erastian" doctrine of the magistrate would fall, not so much because of exegetical support for Presbyterianism as because of the rise of the modern secular state. Although the Synod of Dort was to reject some of Arminius' doctrinal formulations, it followed him in at least two important respects: it rejected the supralapsarianism which Arminius had fought so vigorously, and it affirmed explicitly that the doctrine of predestination must not be understood in such a way that God becomes the author of sin. "The cause or blame for this unbelief, as well as for all other sins, is by no means to be found in God, but rather in man." Also it emphasized that election is "in Christ," a point that Arminius had made emphatically. This is brought out admirably in the new translation of the Canons of Dort by Anthony A. Hoekema in the *Calvin Theological Journal* of November 1968. Dort persisted, however, in making election the ground of the bestowal of faith. Arminius had argued that the doctrine of election does not deal with this issue.

From all of these considerations—the diffuse and complex nature of the early Dutch Reformed Church, the broad and irenic positions of the Belgic Confession and the Heidelberg Catechism, and the central role of Arminius as a Dutch pastor and professor in the life of the Dutch Reformed Church—it is to be concluded that Arminius is indeed one of the theologians of the Dutch Reformed Church and cannot be properly understood under the category of dissenter, outsider, schismatic, or heretic.

221

NOTES

1. For more extended treatments of the situation in Amsterdam, see R. B. Evenhuis, *Ook Dat Was Amsterdam*, I (Amsterdam: W. ten Have, 1965), 51ff., and Carl Bangs, *Arminius: A Study in the Dutch Reformation* (Nashville: Abingdon, 1971), pp. 92ff.

2. G. J. Hoenderdaal, "De Kerkordelijke Kant van de Dordtse Synode," *Nederlands Theologisch Tijdschrift*, XXIII, 5 (June 1969), pp. 349-350.

3. L. Knappert, *Het Ontstaan en de Vestiging van het Protestantisme in de Nederlanden* (Utrecht: A. Oosthoek, 1924), pp. 237-259.

4. Remonstrant writers, understandably, have tended to stress the separate character of the movement, as in F. Pijper, "Geestelijke Stroomingen in Nederland voor de Opkomst van het Remonstrantisme," in G. J. Heering (ed.), *De Remonstranten: Gedenkboek bij het 300-jarig Bestaan der Remonstrantsche Broederschap* (Leiden: A. W. Sijthoff [1919]), pp. 37-59.

5. See O. Fatio, *Nihil Pulchrius Ordine: Contribution à l'Étude de l'Établissement de la Discipline Ecclésiastique aux Pays-Bas* (Leiden: Brill, 1971); and Bangs, *Arminius*, pp. 51-55.

6. Letter to Sebastian Egbertsz, May 3, 1607, in *Praestantium ac eruditorum virorum epistolae ecclesiasticae et theologicae* (Amsterdam, 1660), pp. 236-237 (no. 101 in the 3rd ed., Amsterdam, 1704).

7. Letter to Hippolytus à Collibus, April 5, 1608, in *Praestantium . . .*, p. 928.

8. *Verclaringhe Iacobi Arminii . . .* (Leiden: Thomas Basson, 1610); reprinted in G. J. Hoenderdaal (ed.), *Verklaring van Jacobus Arminius* (Lochem: De Tijdstroom, 1960), pp. 60-61.

9. From the Dutch text of 1562 in J. N. Bakhuizen van den Brink, *De Nederlandsche Belijdenisgeschriften* (Amsterdam: Uitgeversmaatschappij Holland, 1940), p. 89. Here I have corrected an error in my translation of *wtuersien ende verkoren* in my *Arminius*, p. 223, in the light of the French *esleus et choisis*.

10. See the original text of Article 36 in Bakhuizen van den Brink, pp. 135-137.